D0821761

THE JEWISH PEOPLE

HISTORY • RELIGION • LITERATURE

THE JEWISH PEOPLE

HISTORY • RELIGION • LITERATURE

JESUS CHRIST IN THE TALMUD, MIDRASH, ZOHAR,

AND THE

LITURGY OF THE SYNAGOGUE

GUSTAF DALMAN

ARNO PRESS

A New York Times Company

NEW YORK • 1973

Reprint Edition 1973 by Arno Press Inc.

Reprinted from a copy in
  The Princeton Theological Seminary Library

THE JEWISH PEOPLE: History, Religion, Literature
ISBN for complete set: 0-405-05250-2
See last pages of this volume for titles.

Manufactured in the United States of America

————◆————

Library of Congress Cataloging in Publication Data

Dalman, Gustaf Hermann, 1855-1941.
    Jesus Christ in the Talmud, Midrash, Zohar, and
the liturgy of the synagogue.

    (The Jewish people: history, religion, literature)
    Translation of Jesus Christus im Thalmud.
    English and Hebrew.
    Reprint of the 1893 ed. published by Deighton, Bell,
Cambridge.
    1. Jesus Christ--Jewish interpretations.
2. Rabbinical literature--History and criticism.
I. Title. II. Series.
BM620.D313 1973   296.1'206'6   73-2190
ISBN 0-405-05256-1

JESUS CHRIST IN THE TALMUD, MIDRASH, ZOHAR,

AND THE

LITURGY OF THE SYNAGOGUE.

Cambridge:

PRINTED BY C. J. CLAY, M.A., AND SONS,

AT THE UNIVERSITY PRESS.

JESUS CHRIST IN THE TALMUD, MIDRASH, ZOHAR,

AND THE

LITURGY OF THE SYNAGOGUE.

TEXTS AND TRANSLATIONS

BY THE

REV. DR GUSTAF DALMAN,

LECTURER OF THE UNIVERSITY OF LEIPZIG;
DIRECTOR OF THE INSTITUTUM JUDAICUM DELITZSCHIANUM,

TOGETHER WITH AN INTRODUCTORY ESSAY BY

HEINRICH LAIBLE,

MASTER IN THE HIGH SCHOOL OF ROTHENBURG ON TAUBER,

TRANSLATED AND EDITED BY THE

REV. A. W. STREANE, B.D.

FELLOW AND DIVINITY AND HEBREW LECTURER, CORPUS CHRISTI COLLEGE,
AND FORMERLY TYRWHITT'S HEBREW SCHOLAR.

CAMBRIDGE:

DEIGHTON, BELL, AND CO.

LONDON AND NEW YORK: GEORGE BELL & SONS.

1893

PREFACE.

THE attractive subject of Herr Laible's recently published essay ("Jesus Christus im Thalmud") leads me to think that the passages on which he bases his work, and the comments which he makes upon them, cannot be without interest for the English reader, even though the conclusions which he reaches may not on all occasions appear entitled to equally full assent. On my suggesting this to Dr Hermann L. Strack of Berlin (at whose suggestion, as will be seen from the preface to the German edition, Herr Laible undertook the task) I received permission to make use of a large number of spare printed copies of the original texts (numbers I—XXIV; pages 5*—19*) which had been edited by Dr Gustaf H. Dalman of Leipzig. In order to secure in each case the best available (unexpurgated) text, the following editions were used by him.

1.   Palestinian Talmud, Venice, 1523—4.

2.   Babylonian Talmud, Venice. *B'rakhoth, Shabbath, Sota, Gittin, Sanhedrin, 'Aboda zara,* 1520; *Chagigah,* 1521; *Soph'rim,* 1522; *Aboth,* 1526; *'Erubin, Kallah, J'bamoth,* 1528. Variants in the MSS. used by Rabbinovicz (*Dikduke Soph'rim,* or Variae Lectiones in Mischnam et in Talmud Babylonicum, Munich, 1867—1886) are indicated thus: M = the Munich, O = the Oxford, Fl. = the Florence, K = the Karlsruhe MS. For the treatises not dealt with by Rabbinovicz, *'En Ja'akob,* Venice, 1546, was specially used.

3.   *Tosephta,* Zuckermandel, Pasewalk, 1880.

For the present edition Dr Dalman has also supplied a translation (see pages 29*—40*) of the above-mentioned original texts, so far as they do not already appear in Herr Laible's essay; and further, he has now collected from unexpurgated MSS. of Jewish liturgies numerous interesting extracts relating to the same subject (pages 21*—28*) and followed by an English translation (pages 40*—47*).

Hereby, as well as by the introduction of other matter contributed by Dr Dalman and Herr Laible, and incorporated by me with the body of the essay, or appended in the form of foot-notes, the value of this edition of the work is much enhanced.

It has been my aim throughout to render the German as closely as regard for English idiom would permit. At the same time I have ventured to deviate from this rule (a) in dealing with the earlier pages of the essay, which appeared to me to be capable with advantage of some condensation for the English reader, and (b) very occasionally, in modifying expressions used by the Talmud in reference to our Blessed Lord. It may perhaps be considered that I have not gone quite far enough in this latter respect.

Words inserted between square brackets in the text are to be understood in all cases as Herr Laible's. On the other hand all notes for which he is not responsible bear the initials of the writers.

In conclusion I have to express my grateful acknowledgments to the Rev. R. Sinker, D.D., Librarian of Trinity College, for reading the proof-sheets of this work and for many valuable suggestions.

A. W. S.

Inhaltsübersicht.

4*

I. Ben Stada, Ben Pandera, Paphos ben Jehuda, Mirjam die Frauenhaarflechterin. (S. 10.)

a) Schabbath 104ᵇ.

תניא אמר להן רבי אליעזר לחכמים והלא בן סטדא הוציא כשפים
ממצרים בסריטה שעל בשרו אמרו לו שוטה הוה ואין מביאין ראיה מן
השוטים בן סטדא בן פנדירא הוא אמר רב חסדא בעל סטדא בועל
פנדירא בעל פפוס בן יהודה הוא[1] אמו סטדא אמו מרים[2] מגדלא נשיא
הואי[3] כדאמרי בפומבדיתא סטת דא מבעלה:

b) Sanhedrin 67ᵃ.

ושאר כל חייבי מיתות שבתורה אין מכמינין עליהן חוץ מזו כיצד
עושין לו מדליקין לו את הנר בבית הפנימי ומושיבין לו[4] עדים בבית
החיצון כדי שיהו רואין אותו ושומעין את קולו והוא אינו רואה אותן
והלה אומר לו אמור מה שאמרת לי ביחוד והוא אומר לו[5] והלה אומר
לו היאך נניח את אלהינו[6] שבשמים ונעבוד ע״ז אם חוזר בו מוטב
ואם אמר כך היא חובתינו וכך יפה לנו העדים ששומעין מבחוץ
מביאין אותו לבית דין וסוקלין אותו וכן עשו לבן סטדא בלוד ותלאוהו
בערב הפסח. בן סטדא בן פנדירא הוא אמר רב חסדא בעל סטדא
בועל פנדירא בעל פפוס בן יהודה הוא אלא אימא[7] אמו סטדא אמו
מרים מגדלא נשיא[8] הואי כדאמרי בפומבדיתא סטת דא מבעלה:

---

[1] M add. אלא ‖ [2] so auch O; M om. ‖ [3] M add. אלא ‖ [4] M
om. לו ‖ [5] M om. והוא אומר לו ‖ [6] M אבינו ‖ [7] M om. אימא ‖
[8] M נשיא

II. Karikatur von „Evangelium". (S. 14, vgl. 65.)

Schabbath 116ᵃ (nach Ms. München).

רבי מאיר קרי ליה און גליון ר' יוחנן קרי ליה עון גליון:

III. Das Weib des Paphos ben Jehuda. (S. 26.)

Gittin 90ᵃ (vgl. Thosephtha Sota V,).

תניא היה ר״מ אומר כשם שהדעות במאכל כך דעות בנשים יש
לך אדם שזבוב נופל לתוך כוסו וזרקו ואינו שותהו וזו היא מדת פפוס
בן יהודה שהיה נועל בפני אשתו ויוצא ויש לך אדם שזבוב נופל לתוך
כוסו וזורקו ושותהו וזו היא מדת כל אדם שמדברת עם אחיה וקרוביה
ומניחה ויש לך אדם שזבוב נופל לתוך תמחוי מוצצו ואוכלו זו היא
מדת אדם רע שרואה את אשתו יוצאה וראשה פרוע וטווה בשוק
ופרומה משני צדדיה ורוחצת עם בני אדם:

רש״י: פפוס בן יהודה בעלה של מרים מגדלא נשיא וכשיצא
מביתו לשוק נעל דלת בפניה שלא תדבר לכל אדם ומדה שאינה
הוגנת היא זו שמתוך כך איבה נכנסת ביניהם ומזנה תחתיו:

IV. Marienlegende. (S. 28.)

a) Chagiga 4ᵇ.

רב יוסף כי מטי להאי קרא בכי ויש נספה בלא משפט אמר מי
איכא דאזיל בלא זמניה אין כי הא דרב ביבי[1] בר אביי הוה שכיח
גביה מלאך המות אמר ליה[2] לשלוחיה זיל אייתי לי[3] מרים מגדלא שיער[4]
נשיא אזל אייתי ליה מרים מגדלא דרדקי אמר ליה אנא מרים מגדלא
שיער[5] נשיא אמרי לך אמר ליה אי הכי[6] אהדרה[7] אמר ליה הואיל ואייתיתה
ליהוי[8] למניינא:

b) Thosaphoth Chagiga 4ᵇ. (S. 30.)

האי עובדא דמרים מגדלא נשיא בבית שני היה דהיתה אמו של
פלוני[9] כדאיתא בשבת:

[1] M om. דימי || [2] M om. ליה || [3] M om. לי || [4] M om. שיער || [5] M om.
ישו 'En Ja'aqob || [6] M om. א״ל אי הכי || [7] M אהדרינה || [8] M תיהוי || [9] M om. שיער

c) Thosaphoth Schabbath 104[b] (vgl. S. 30).

בן סטדא אור"ת דאין זה ישו הנוצרי דהא בן סטדא אמרינן הכא
דהוה בימי פפוס בן יהודה דהוה דהוה בימי ר' עקיבא כדמוכח בפ' בתרא
דברכות וישו היה בימי יהושע בן פרחיה כדמוכח בפ' בתרא דסוטה
ולא כר' יהושע בן פרחיה שדחה לישו הנוצרי בשתי ידים ור' יהושע
הוה קדים טובא לר' עקיבא: אמו מרים מגדלא נשיא היא והא דקאמר
בפר' קמא דחגיגה רב ביבי הוה שכיח גביה מלאך המות כו' אמר ליה
לשלוחיה זיל אייתי לי מרים מגדלה נשי' משמע שהיתה בימי רב ביבי
מרים מגדלא נשיא אחרת היתה אי נמי מלאך המות היה מספר לרב
ביבי מעשה שאירע כבר מזמן גדול:

V. Mirjam Tochter Bilga's. (S. 21 Anm.)

pal. Sukka 55[d].

בלגה לעולם חולקת בדרום מפני מרים בת בלגה שנשתמדה
והלכה ונישאת לסרדיוט אחד משל מלכות בית יון ובאה וטפחה על
גגו של מזבח אמרה לו לוקום לוקום אתה החרבתה נכסיהן של
ישראל ולא עמדת להן בשעת דוחקן:

VI. Die jerusalemische Urkunde. (S. 31.)

Jebamoth 49[a], Mischna IV, 13.

אמ' ר"ש בן עזאי מצאתי מגלת יוחסין בירושלם וכתוב בה איש
פלוני ממזר מאשת איש:

VII. Die Selbstaussage der Maria. (S. 33.)

Kalla 18[b] (41[c] ed. Ven. 1528).

(mit den Varianten der Ausgabe von N. Coronel: חמשה קונטרסים Commentarios quinque doctrinam talmudicam illustrantes, Massekheth Kala . . . .
edidit Nathan Coronel, Wien 1864, Bl. 3[b].)

עז פנים ר' אליעזר אומר ממזר ר' יהושע אומר בן הנדה ר'
עקיבא אומר ממזר ובן הנדה*. פעם אחת היו זקנים יושבים בשער[1]
ועברו[2] לפניהם שתי[3] תינוקות אחד כסה[4] את ראשו ואחד גילה[5] את

* Zusatz. ‖ [1] om. בשער ‖ [2] עברו ‖ [3] שני ‖ [4] גלה ‖ [5] כסא

ראשו זה שגילה אתו[1] ראשו אליעזר אומר ממזר ר' יהושע אומר בן
הנדה ר' עקיבא אומר ממזר ובן הנדה . אמרו לו לר'[2] עקיבא היאך[3]
מלאך לבך לעבור על דברי חבריך? אמר להן[4] זה[5] אני אקיימנו.
הלך אצל אמו של[6] תינוק וראה[7] שהיתה[8] יושבת ומוכרת קיטנית[9]
בשוק . אמר לה בתי אם את אומרת[10] לי דברי[11] שאני שואלך[12] אני[13]
מביאך לחיי עולם[14] הבא . אמרה לו השבע לי . היה ר' עקיבא נשבע
בשפתיו[15] ומבטל[16] בלבו, אמר לה בנך[17] זה מה טיבו? אמרה לו
כשנכנסתי לחופה נדה הייתי ופירש ממני בעלי ובא עלי[18] שושביני
והיה[19] לי בן זה . נמצא התינוק[20] ממזר ובן הנדה . אמרו גדול היה ר'
עקיבא שהוביש[21] את רבותיו . באותה[22] שעה אמרו ברוך ה' אלהי
ישראל אשר גילה[23] סודו לר' עקיבא[24] בן יוסף:

VIII. Jesus und Jehoschuaʿ ben Perachja. (S. 40.)

a) Sanhedrin 107ᵇ.

תנו רבנן לעולם תהא שמאל דוחה וימין מקרבת לא כאלישע
שדחפו לגחזי בשתי ידים[25] ולא כרבי[26] יהושע[26] בן פרחיה שדחפו לישו[27]
בשתי ידים[28] גחזי דכתיב . . . .ר' יהושע בן פרחיה מאי היא כדקטלינהו[29]
ינאי מלכא לרבנן אזל רבי[30] יהושע בן פרחיה וישו[31] לאלכסנדריא של
מצרים כי הוה שלמא שלח ליה שמעון בן שטח מיני ירושלם[32] עיר
הקודש ליכי אלכסנדריא של מצרים אחותי[33] בעלי שרוי בתוכך ואנכי
יושבת שוממה. קם אתא ואתרמי ליה[34] ההוא[35] אושפיזא עבדו ליה
יקרא טובא אמר כמה יפה אכסניא זו אמר ליה[36] רבי עיניה טרוטות
אמר ליה רשע בכך אתה עוסק אפיק ארבע מאות שיפורי ושמתיה אתא
לקמיה כמה זימנין אמר ליה קבלן לא הוה קא משגח ביה יומא חד

¹ om. את ‖ ² om. ‖ ³ איך ‖ ⁴ להם ‖ ⁵ om. ‖ ⁶ add. אותו
אומר לך ¹² ‖ זה add. ¹¹ ‖ תאמר ¹⁰ ‖ קטנית ⁹ ‖ שהיא ⁸ ‖ ומצאה ⁷
ובעלני ¹⁸ ‖ בנך ¹⁷ ‖ לו ¹⁶ ‖ add. בשפתותיו ¹⁵ ‖ העולם ¹⁴ ‖ הריני ¹³
ברוך שגלה ²³ ‖ באותו ²² ‖ שהכחיש ²¹ ‖ אותו תינוק ²⁰ ‖ ועברתי את זה ¹⁹
ידיו M ²⁸ ‖ לישו הנוצרי M ²⁷ ‖ כיהושע M ²⁶ ‖ ידיו M ²⁵ ‖ לעקיבא ²⁴
ירושלם M om. ³² ‖ ישו M om. ³¹ ‖ רבי M om. ³⁰ ‖ דכי קטלינהו M ²⁹
אמר ליה ישו M ³⁶ ‖ בההוא M ³⁵ ‖ ליה M om. ³⁴ ‖ אחותי M om. ³³

הוה קא קרי קרית שמע אתא לקמיה סבר לקבולי אחוי להו[1] בידיה
הוא סבר מידחא דחי ליה אזל זקף לבינתא והשתחוה לה אמר ליה
הדר בך אמר ליה כך מקובלני ממך כל החוטא ומחטיא את הרבים
אין מספיקין בידו לעשות תשובה ואמר מר ישו[2] כישף והסית והדיח
את ישראל:

b) Sota 47ª.

לא כאלישע שדחפו לגחזי בשתי ידיו ולא כיהושע בן פרחיה
שדחפו לישו הנוצרי בשתי ידיו אלישע מאי היא ...... יהושע בן
פרחיה מאי היא כדהוה קא קטיל ינאי מלכא לרבנן שמעון בן שטח
אטמינהו אחתיה רבי יהושע בן פרחיה אזל ערק לאלכסנדריא של
מצרים כי הוה שלמא שלח ליה שמעון בן שטח מני ירושלם עיר הקודש
לך אלכסנדריא של מצרים אחותי בעלי שרוי בתוכך ואני יושבת שוממה
אמר ש״מ הוה ליה שלמא כי אתא איקלעו לההוא אושפיזא קם קמייהו
ביקרא שפיר עבדי ליה יקרא טובא יתיב וקא משתבח כמה נאה
אכסניא זו אמר ליה רבי עיניה טרוטות אמר ליה רשע בכך אתה
עוסק אפיק ארבע מאה שיפורי ושמתיה כל יומא אתא לקמיה ולא
קבליה יומא חד הוה קרי קרית שמע אתא לקמיה הוה בדעתיה לקבוליה
אחוי ליה בידיה סבר מידחא דחי ליה אזל זקף לבינתא פלחא אמר
ליה חזור בך אמר ליה כך מקובלני ממך כל החוטא ומחטיא את
הרבים אין מספיקין בידו לעשות תשובה:*

c) pal. Chagiga 77ᵈ.

יהודה בן טבאי הוון בני ירושלם בעון ממניתיה נשיא בירושלם.
ערק ואזל ליה לאלכסנדריאה והיו בני ירושלם כותבין מירושלם הגדולה
לאלכסנדריאה הקטנה עד מתי ארוסי יושב אצלכם ואני יושבת עגומה
עליו. פירש מיתי גו אילפא אמר דבורה מרתה דביתא דקבלתן מה
הוות חסירה. אמר ליה חד מן תלמידוי רבי עיינה הוות שברה. א״ל
הא תרתי גבך. חדא דחשדתני וחדא דאיסתכלת בה מה אמרית יאייא
בריוא. לא אמרית אלא בעובדא. וכעס עליו ואזל:

מאי עבד דאמר מר :.En Jaʿaqob add* ‖ ישו הנוצרי M ² ‖ ליה M ¹
ישו הנוצרי כישף והסית והדיח והחטיא את ישראל:

IX. Der Zauberer Jesus. (S. 45.)

a) Schabbath 104[b] s. oben Nr. I.

b) Thosephtha Schabbath XII g. E. (ed. Zuckermandel S. 126).

המסרט על בשרו ר' אליעזר מחייב וחכמים פוטרין אמר להם ר'
אליעזר והלא בן סטדא לא למד אלא בכך אמרו לו מפני שוטה אחד
נאבד את כל הפיקחין:

c) pal. Schabbath 13[d].

הקורע על העור כתבנית כתב חייב הרושם על העור כתבנית
כתב פטור אמר להן רבי אליעזר והלא בן סטדא לא הביא כשפים
ממצרים אלא בכך אמרו לו מפני שוטה אחד אנו מאבדין כמה פיקחין:

X. Das Selbstzeugnis Jesu. (S. 48f.)

a) pal. Tha'anith 65[b].

אמר רבי אבהו אם יאמר לך אדם אל אני מכזב הוא בן אדם
אני סופו לתהות בו שאני עולה לשמים ההוא אמר ולא יקימינה:

b) Jalqut Schim'oni (Salonichi 1526) zu 4 Mos. 23, 7, nach Midrasch
J'lamm'denu.

מברך רעהו בקול גדול כמה היה קולו של בלעם ר' יוחנן אמר
ששים מילין ר' יהושע בן לוי אמר שבעים אומות שמעו קולו של בלעם
ר' אליעזר הקפר אומר נתן האלהים כח בקולו והיה עולה מסוף העולם
ועד סופו בשביל שהיה צופה וראה האומות שמשתחוין לשמש וירח
ולכוכבים ולעץ ולאבן¹ וצפה וראה שיש אדם בן אשה שעתיד לעמוד
שמבקש לעשות עצמו אלוה ולהטעות כל העולם כלו לפי' נתן כח שקולו
בקולו .l] שישמעו כל אומות העולם² וכן היה אומר תנו דעתיכם שלא

¹ Ed. Frankf. 1687 om. אלוה--וכן ‖ וצפה--כלו ² Ed. Frankf. om. אלוה
S. auch Bechaj zu 4 Mose 23,19 (Pesaro 1507) ויכזב אל איש לא ובמדרש
לפי שצפה בלעם שעתיד אדם אחד להטעות את העולם ולומר שהוא אלוה התחיל צווח
איש נעשה אלוה עתיד הוא להתנחם ואומר דבר ואינו יכול לעשותו שנאמר ההוא אמר
ולא יעשה:

לטעות אחרי אותו האיש שנא׳ לא איש אל ויכזב ואם אומר שהוא
אל הוא מכזב והוא עתיד להטעות ולומר שהוא מסתלק ובא לקיצים
ההוא אמר ולא יעשה ראה מה כתיב וישא משלו ויאמר אוי מי יחיה
משומו אל אמר בלעם אוי מי יחיה מאותה אומה ששמעה אחר אותו
האיש שעשה עצמו אלוה:

c) Pesiqtha Rabbathi 100ᵇ (Ausg. Friedmann).

אמר ר׳ חייא בר אבא אם יאמר לך ברא דזניתא תרין אלהים
אינון אימר ליה אנא הוא דימא אנא הוא דסיני .... אמר ר׳ חייא
בר אבא אם יאמר לך ברא דזניתא תרין אלהים אינון אימא ליה פנים
בפנים דברו אלהים אין כתב כאן אלא דבר ה׳ עמכם:

XI. Jesus, ein Götzendiener. (S. 49.)

a) Sanhedrin 103ᵃ.

לא תאונה אליך רעה שלא יבעתוך חלומות רעים והרהורים ונגע
לא יקרב באהלך שלא יהא לך בן או תלמיד שמקדיח תבשילו ברבים
כגון ישו הנוצרי:

b) Berakhoth 18ᵃ.

כי הוו מפטרי רבנן מבי רב חסדא ואמרי לה מבי רב שמואל
בר נחמני אמרו[1] ליה הכי אלופינו מסובלי[2] רב ושמואל ואמרי לה
ר׳ יוחנן ור׳ אלעזר חד אמר אלופינו בתורה ומסבלים במצות וחד אמר
אלופינו בתורה ובמצות ומסבלים ביסורים אין פרץ שלא תהא סיעתינו
כסיעתו של שאול שיצא ממנו דואג האדומי ואין יוצאת שלא תהא
סיעתינו כסיעתו של דוד שיצא ממנו אחיתופל ואין צוחה שלא תהא
סיעתינו כסיעתו של אלישע שיצא ממנו גחזי ברחובותינו שלא יהא
לנו בן או תלמיד שמקדיח[3] תבשילו ברבים כגון[4] הנוצרי:

אין פרץ ואין יוצאת ואין צוחה ברחובותינו מאי אלופינו .add M [2] ‖ אמרי M [1]
מסובלים M [3] ‖ שיקדיח M [4] ‖ .add M ‖ ישו

XII. Bileam-Jesus. (S. 51f.)

a) Sanhedrin XI, 90ª; Mischna X, 2.

שלשה מלכים וארבעה הדיוטות אין להן חלק לעולם הבא שלשה
מלכים ירבעם אחאב ומנשה רבי יהודה אומר מנשה יש לו חלק לעולם
הבא שנאמר ויתפלל אליו וישמע תחינתו וישיבהו ירושלם למלכותו
אמרו לו למלכותו השיבו ולא לחיי העולם הבא השיבו ארבע הדיוטות
בלעם ודואג ואחיתופל וגחזי:

α) Sanhedrin XI, 90ª; Mischna X, 1 (S. 52 u. 53).

ר' עקיבא אומר אף הקורא בספרים החיצונים והלוחש על המכה
ואומר כל המחלה אשר שמתי במצרים לא אשים עליך כי אני יי' רופאך:

β) Sanhedrin 100ᵇ (vgl. S. 53).

אף הקורא בספר החיצונים וכו' תנא בספרי מינים:

b) Aboth V, 19 (S. 55).

תלמידיו של בלעם הרשע יורשין גיהנם ויורדין לבאר שחת שנ
ואתה אלהים תורידם לבאר שחת אנשי דמים ומרמה לא יחצו ימיהם
ואני אבטח בך:

c) Sanhedrin 106ᵇ.

אמר ליה ההוא מינא לרבי חנינא מי שמיע לך בלעם בר כמה
הוה אמר ליה מיכתב לא כתיב אלא מדכתיב אנשי דמים ומרמה לא
יחצו ימיהם או בר תלתין ותלת שנין או בר תלתין וארבע אמר ליה
שפיר קאמרת לדידי חזי לי פנקסיה דבלעם הוה כתיב ביה בר תלתין
ותלת שנין בלעם חגירא כד קטילתיה¹ פנחס ליסטאה:

d) Sanhedrin 106ᵇ Ende (S. 56).

אמר רבי יוחנן דואג ואחיתופל לא חצו ימיהם תניא נמי הכי
אנשי דמים ומרמה לא יחצו ימיהם כל שנותיו של דואג לא היו אלא
שלשים וארבע ושל אחיתופל אינן אלא שלשים ושלש:

¹ Fl. קטל יתיה

e) Sanhedrin 106ᵃ (S. 58).

אוי מי יחיה משמו אל אמר ריש לקיש אוי מי¹ שמחיה עצמו
בשם אל:

רש״י: בלעם שמחייה עצמו בשם אלוה עושה עצמו אלוה
ל״א מי שמחיה עצמו בשם אל כלומר אוי להם לאותן בני אדם שמחיין
ומעדנין עצמן בעולם הזה ופורקין עול תורה מעל צואר׳ ומשניין² את
עצמן:

XIII. R. Eliʿezer und Jaʿaqob von Kephar Sekhanja. (S. 58f.)

a) ʿAboda zara 16ᵇ, 17ᵃ.

תנו רבנן כשנתפס רבי אליעזר³ למינות העלוהו לגרדום לידון
אמר לו אותו הגמון זקן שכמותך יעסק בדברים בטילים הללו אמ׳ לו
נאמן עלי הדיין כסבור אותו הגמון עליו הוא אומר והוא לא אמר
אלא כנגד¹ אביו שבשמים אמר לו הואיל והאמנתי עליך⁵ דימוס פטור
אתה כשבא לביתו נכנסו תלמידיו אצלו לנחמו ולא קיבל עליו תנחומי׳
אמ׳ לו רבי עקיבא רבי תרשיני לומר דבר אחד ממה שלימדתני אמר
ליה אמור אמר לו רבי שמא מינות בא לידך והנאך ועליו נתפסת
למינות אמ׳ לו עקיבה הזכרתני פעם אחת הייתי מהלך בשוק העליון
של ציפורי ומצאתי אחד⁶ מתלמידי ישו הנוצרי ויעקב איש כפר סכניא
שמו אמר לי כתוב בתורתכם לא תביא אתנן זונה מהו לעשות הימנו⁷
בית הכסא לכהן גדול ולא אמרתי לו כלום אמר לי כך לימדני ישו
הנוצרי מאתנן זונה קובצה עד אתנן זונה ישוב ממקום הטנופת באו
למקום⁸ הטנופת⁹ ילכו והנאני הדבר על ידי זה¹⁰ נתפסתי למינות
ועברתי על מה שכתוב בתורה הרחק מעליה דרכך זו מינות ואל תקרב
אל פתח ביתה זו הרשות ואיכא דאמרי הרחק מעלי׳ דרכך זו מינות
והרשות ואל תקרב אל פתח ביתה זו זונה:

---

¹ Jalqut Schim. Salonichi 1526 למי ‖ ² ʾEn Jaʿaqob ‖ ³ M
מהן M ⁷ ‖ אדם אחד M ⁶ ‖ והאמנת עלי M ⁵ ‖ לאביו M ⁴ ‖ הגדול .add
ועליו M ¹⁰ ‖ ישובו .M add ⁹ ‖ עד מקום M ⁸

14*

מעשה ברבי אליעזר שנתפס לשום מינות נטלו אותו הגמון והעלו
על הבימה לדון אותו אמר לו רבי אדם גדול כמותך יעסוק בדברים
בטלים הללו אמר לו נאמן עלי הדיין והוא סבר שבשבילו אמר והוא
לא אמר אלא לשום שמים אמר לו מאחר שהאמנתי עליך אף אני
הייתי סבור ואומר אפשר שישיבות הללו טועות הן בדברים בטלים
הללו דימוס פטור אתה אחר שנפטר רבי אליעזר מן הבימה היה
מצטער על שנתפש בצד מינות על דברי מינות נכנסו תלמידיו
אצלו לנחמו ולא קבל נכנס רבי עקיבא אצלו א"ל רבי שמא אחד
מן המינין אמר לפניך דבר וערב לפניך אמר לו הן השמים הזכרתני
פעם אחת הייתי עולה באיסטרטא של צפרי ובא אלי אדם אחד ויעקב
איש כפר סכניא שמו ואמר לי דבר אחד משום ישו בן פנדרא[1] והנאני
הדבר ואותו הדבר היה כתוב בתורתכם לא תביא אתנן זונה ומחיר
כלב מה הן אמרתי לו אסורין. אמר לי לקרבן אסורין לאבדן מותר
אמרתי לו ואם כן מה יעשה בהם אמ' לי יעשה בהן בתי מרחצאות
ובתי כסאות אמרתי לו יפה אמרת ונתעלמה ממני הלכה לשעה. כיון
שראה שהודתי לדבריו אמר לי כך אמר בן פנדרא מצואה באו ולצואה
יצאו שנ' כי מאתנן זונה קבצה ועד אתנן זונה ישובו יעשו כורסוון
לרבים והנאני ועל אותו הדבר נתפשתי לשם מינות ולא עוד אלא
שעברתי על מה שכתוב בתורה הרחק מעליה דרכך ..... זו המינות:

XIV. Imma Salome, Rabban Gamliel und der „Philosoph". (S. 62f.)

Schabbath 116[ab]

אימא שלום דביתהו דרבי אליעזר אחתיה דרבן גמליאל הואי הוה
ההוא פילוסופא[2] בשבבותיה דהוה שקיל שמא דלא מקבל שוחדא בעו
לאחוכי ביה אעיילא ליה שרגא דדהבא ואזול[3] לקמיה אמרה ליה בעינא
דניפלגי לי בנכסי דבי נשי אמר להו פלוגו א"ל כתיב לן[4] במקום ברא
ברתא לא תירות א"ל מן יומא דגליתון מארעכון איתנטלי[’] אורייתא

---

[1] Thosephtha Chullin II,24 (ed. Zuckermandel S. 503): ישוע בן
באורייתא M [4] ‖ ואזלה M [3] ‖ פלנספא קבא M [2] ‖ פנטי״י

דמשה ואיתיהיבת[1] עון גיליון וכתיב ביה ברא וברתא כחדא ירתון
למחר הדר עייל ליה איהו חמרא לובא אמר להו שפילית[2] לסיפיה
דעון גיליון וכת' ביה אנא עון גיליון לא למיפח[3] מאורייתא דמשה
אתיתי אלא לאוספי על אוריתא דמשה[4] אתיתי וכתיב ביה במקום
ברא ברתא לא תירות אמרה ליה נהור נהוריך כשרגא א"ל רבן גמליאל
אתא חמרא ובטש לשרגא:

XV. Die 5 Jünger Jesu. (S. 66 f.)

Sanhedrin 43ᵃ.

והתניא בערב הפסח[5] תלאוהו לישו[6] והכרוז יוצא לפניו מ' יום[7]
יוצא ליסקל על[8] שכישף והסית והדיח את ישראל כל מי שיודע לו
זכות יבא וילמד עליו ולא מצאו לו זכות ותלאוהו בערב פסח[9] אמר עולא
ותסברא בר הפוכי זכות הוא מסית הוא[10] ורחמנא אמר לא תחמול ולא
תכסה עליו אלא שאני ישו[11] דקרוב למלכות הוה. ת"ר חמשה תלמידים
היו לו לישו מתאי נקאי נצר ובוני ותודה אתיוה למתי אמר להו מתי
יהרג הכתיב מתי אבוא ואראה פני אלקים אמרו לו אין מתי יהרג דכתיב
מתי ימות ואבד שמו אתיוה לנקאי אמר להו נקאי יהרג הכתיב ונקי
וצדיק אל תהרוג אין נקאי יהרג דכתיב במסתרים יהרג נקי אתיוה לנצר
אמר נצר יהרג דכתיב ונצר משרשיו יפרה אמרו ליה אין נצר יהרג דכתיב
ואתה השלכת מקברך כנצר נתעב אתיוה לבוני אמר בוני יהרג הכתיב
בני בכורי ישראל אמרו לו אין בוני יהרג דכתיב הנה אנכי הרג את
בנך בכורך אתיוה לתודה אמר תודה יהרג הכתיב מזמור לתודה א"ל
אין תודה יהרג דכתיב זובח תודה יכבדנני:

XVI. Der wunderthätige Jaʿaqob aus Kephar Sekhanja. (S. 72.)

a) pal. Schabbath 14ᵈ unten.

מעשה בר' אלעזר בן דמה שנשכו נחש ובא יעקב איש כפר סמא[12]
משם של ישו פנדירא[13] לרפותו[14] ולא הניח לו רבי ישמעאל. אמר לו

למיפק [1] ואיתיהבית ביה M ‖ [2] שפילי ליה M O ‖ [3] ʿEn Jaʿaqob
הנוצרי M add. ‖ [4] M om. על אורית' דמשה ‖ [5] Fl בערב שבת ובערב הפסח ‖ [6] M add.
ותסברא M [10] ‖ Fl בערב שבת ובערב הפסח [9] ‖ ליסקל M [8] ‖ ישו הנוצרי M add. [7]
כפר סמא [12] ‖ הנוצרי M add. [11] ‖ ישו הנוצרי בר הפוכי ליה זכות הוה מסית הוה
auch pal. ʿAb. zara 40ᵈ u. Thosephtha Chullin II,23 ‖ [13] Thosephtha
אמר לו נימא לך בשם ישו בן פנדרא pal. ʿAb. zara 40ᵈ add. ‖ [14] ישוע בן פנטרא

אני מביא ראייה שירפאני. לא הספיק להביא ראייה עד שמת בן דמה.
אמר לו ר' ישמעאל אשריך בן דמה שיצאת בשלום מן העולם ולא
פרצתה גדירן של חכמים דכתיב ופורץ גדר ישכנו נחש ולא נחש נשכו
אלא שלא ישכנו נחש לעתיד לבוא:

b) bab. ʿAboda zara 27[b].

מעשה בבן דמא בן אחותו של רבי ישמעאל שהכישו נחש ובא
יעקב[1] איש סכניא[2] לרפאותו[3] ולא הניחו רבי ישמעאל ואמר לו ר'
ישמעאל אחי הנח לו וארפא ממנו ואני אביא מקרא מן התורה שהוא
מותר ולא הספיק לגמור את הדבר עד שיצתה נשמתו ומת[4] קרא עליו
ר' ישמעאל אשריך בן דמא שגופך טהור ויצתה נשמתך בטהרה ולא
עברת על דברי חביריך:

XVII. Noch ein wunderthätiger Christ. (S. 48, Z. 11; S. 71 ff.)

a) pal. ʿAboda zara 40[d] (Varianten aus pal. Schabbath 14[d]).

בר בריה[0] הוה ליה בלע אתא חד[5] ולחש ליה בשמיה דישו בן[6]
פנדרא ואינשם מנפק[7] אמר ליה מאי[8] אמרת עלייה[8] אמר ליה למילת
פלן. אמר[9] מה[10] הוה ליה אילו מית[11] ולא[12] שמע הדא מלתא.א[12] והוות
ליה כן כשגגה שיוצא מלפני השליט:

b) Qoheleth rabba zu 10,5 (Pesaro 1519).

בריה דרבי יהושע בן לוי הוה ליה חד בלעא אזל ואייתי חד מן
אילין דבר פנדירא לאפקא בלעיה אמר ליה מה אמרת עלוי. אמר ליה
פסוק פלן בתר פלן. אמר הוה נייח ליה דקבריה ולא הוה אמר עלוי
הדין פסוקא, וכן הות ליה כשגגה שיוצא מלפני השליט:

[1] M מינא יעקב ‖ [2] M כפר סכניא Qohel. rabba zu 1,8 כפר שכניא
[3] Qoh. rabba add. משום ישו בן פנדר' ‖ [4] M om. ומת ‖ [0] Nach dem
Vorausgehenden der Enkel des Josua ben Levi. ‖ [5] חד בר נש ‖ [6] om.
הוה מיית [11] ‖ ניח [10] ‖ אמר ליה [9] ‖ מאן לחשתה ליה [8] ‖ כד נפק [7] ‖ בן
ולא כן [12]

XVIII. Jesu Verurteilung. (S. 73 f.)

a) Sanhedrin 67ᵃ (s. oben No. I.)

b) pal. Sanhedrin 25ᶜᵈ.

המסית זה ההדיוט. כו' הא חכם לא מכיון שהוא מסית אין זה חכם
מכיון שהוא גיסית אין זה חכם כיצד עושין לו להעריס עליו מכמינין
עליו שני עדים בבית הפנימי ומושיבין אותו בבית החיצון ומדליקין את
הנר על גביו כדי שיהו רואין אותו ושומעין את קולו כך¹ עשו לבן
סוטדה² בלוד והכמינו עליו שני תלמידי חכמים והביאוהו לבית דין
וסקלוהו:

XIX. Jesu Hinrichtung.

Sanhedrin 43ᵃ (s. oben No. XV).

XX. Die Lehrhalle des Ben Pandera. (S. 83.)

Thargum scheni zu Esther 7,9 (Venedig 1591).

וכד חזא המן דלא משתמעין מילוי נטל איליא וביתא על נפשיה
במציעות גינת ביתנא. מתיב וכן אמר אציתו לי אילניא וכל שתיליא די
שתלית מן יומי בראשית דבר המדתא בעי מיסוק לאכסנדריא דבר
פנדירא.

XXI. Jesus in der Hölle. (S. 84 f.)

a) Gittin 56ᵇ, 57ᵃ.

אנקלוס בר קלוניקוס בר אחתיה דטיטוס הוה בעי לאיגיורי אזל
אסקיה לטיטוס בנגידא א"ל מאן חשיב בההוא עלמא א"ל ישראל מהו
לאידבוקי בהו א"ל מילייהו נפישין ולא מצית לקיימינהו זיל איגדי³ בהו
בההוא עלמא והוית רישא דכתיב היו צריה לראש וגו' כל המיצר לישראל
נעשה ראש א"ל דיניה דההוא גברא במאי א"ל במאי דפסיק אנפשיה
כל יומא מכנסי ליה לקיטמיה ודייני ליה וקלו ליה ומבדרו אשב ימי אזל
אסקיה לבלעם בנגידא אמר ליה מאן חשיב בההוא עלמא אמר ליה

---

¹ pal. Jebamoth 15ᵈ שכן ‖ ² ebenda לבן סטרא ‖ ³ 'En Ja'aqob אגרי

ישראל מהו לאידבוקי בהו אמר ליה לא תדרוש שלומם וטובתם כל
הימים אמר ליה דיניה דההוא גברא במאי א"ל בשכבת זרע רותחת
אזל אסקיה לישו¹ בנגידא אמ' ליה מאן חשיב בההוא עלמא אמר ליה
ישראל מהו לאידבוקי בהו א"ל טובתם דרוש רעתם לא תדרוש כל
הנוגע בהן כאילו נוגע בבבת עינו אמר ליה דיניה דההוא גברא במאי
אמר ליה בצואה רותחת דאמר מר כל המלעיג על דברי חכמים נידון
בצואה רותחת תא חזי מה בין פושעי ישראל לנביאי אומות העולם:

b) Thosaphoth zu ʿErubin 21ᵇ

„מי כתיב לעג" מכל מקום אמת הוא שנדון בצואה רותחת כדאמרין
בהנזקין גבי ישו הנוצרי:

XXII. Mirjam, Tochter des ʿEli, in der Hölle. (S. 30.)

pal. Chagiga 77ᵈ (mit Varianten aus pal. Sanhedrin 23ᶜ).

וחמא למרים ברת² עלי בצלים רבי לעזר בר יוסה אמר³ תלייא
בחיטי ביזייא ר' יוסי בן חנינא אמר צירא דתרעא⁴ דגיהנם קביע באודנה
אמר לון למה דא כן אמר ליה דהוות ציימה ומפרסמה ואית דאמרי
דהוות ציימה חד יום ומקזה ליה תריי⁵ אמר לון עד אימת היא כן אמ'
ליה עד דייתי שמעון בן שטח ואנן מרימין לה מן גו אודנה וקבעין ליה
גו אודניה:

XXIII. Jesus, Pilatus und Herodes, Vorfahren Hamans. (vgl. S. 29 u. 81.)

Sophʾrim XIII, 6; Varianten aus Targum scheni zu Esther 3,1, Ven. 1591.

בתר פתגמיא האילין רבי מלכא אחשורוש ית המן בן המדתא אגגא⁶
בר כוזא⁷ בר אפוליטוס⁸ בר דיוס⁹ בר דיוסוס¹⁰ בר פרוס¹¹ בר נידן¹² בר

רבי לעזר בר יוסה אמר om. ³ ‖ בת ² ‖ En Jaʿaqob add. הנוצרי ¹
אמר לון למה om. ⁵ ‖ ר' יוסי בן חנינא אמר צירא דתרעא statt ואית דמרין תרעא ⁴
דיוסים ¹⁰ ‖ דיוסף ⁹ ‖ איפלוטם ⁸ ‖ בוזה ⁷ ‖ אגגיא בר סרח ⁶ ‖ תריי bis דא כן
מעדן ¹² ‖ פדום ¹¹

בעלקן' בר אוטימרוס² בר הדוס³ בר הדורוס בר שגר בר נגר בר
פרמישתא בר ויזתא⁵ בר עמלק בר לחינתיה" דאליפז בוכריה דעישו :

XXIV. Anhang: Jesus im Zohar. (S. 2.)

Zohar III, 282ª (Ra'jâ mehêmnâ).

Die Stelle ist verstümmelt in den ersten Ausgaben des Zohar, Mantua
und Cremona 1560, wird nach einer orientalischen Quelle ergänzt von
Mose Zakuth in Derekh Emeth (o. J. u. O. — nach Wolf, um 1663),
erscheint zum ersten Mal vollständig im Text in Ausg. Konstantinopel
1736. Hier wird sie nach Ausg. Mantua 1560 und Derekh Emeth mit-
geteilt. Die in Ausg. Mantua ausgelassenen Stellen sind durch Klammern
eingefasst.

מסטרא דעבודה זרה אתקריאת שבתאי לילית אשפה מעורבת בגין
דצואה מעורבת מכל מיני טנוף ושרץ דזרקין בה כלבים מתים וחמורים
מתים בני עשו וישמעאל רבה⁷ י"שו ומח"מד] דאינון כלבים מתים [קבורים
בהו⁸ איהי קבר דעבודה זרה דקברין לון ערלים⁹ כלבים מתים] שקץ וריה
רע מטונף מסורח משפחה בישא איהי סרכא דאחידא בערב רב מעורבים
בישראל ואחידת בעצם ובשר דאינון [בני עשו וישמעאל] עצם מת ובשר
טמא בשר בשדה טרפה ועלה אתמר לכלב תשליכון אותו :

---

¹ בלעקן ‖ ² אנתימרום ‖ ³ om. ‖ ⁴ הרידום ‖ ⁵ Tharg. scheni,
Amst. 1670 add. בר אגג בר סומקי ‖ ⁶ לחינתה — Vgl. noch Joel Müller,
Masechet Soferim, Leipzig 1878 S. XXII, Einl. S. 34, Anmerkungen S. 176.
Der von Müller für diese Stelle gegebene Text ist ohne handschriftliche
Bezeugung. ‖ ⁷ Ausg. Konstant. 1736 קבורים בה ‖ ⁸ בה ‖ ⁹ add.
דאינון

XXV. JESUS IN THE LITURGY OF THE SYNAGOGUE.

[This did not appear in the German edition.]

In mediaeval Jewish prayers Jesus is called נצר נתעב (cp. Is. xiv. 19), פגר מת, הכלב המת, טמא ומת, מת, צלב, תלוי, נצר נפוף, ייחום אישת הזימה, עול הזימה, ילוד ואמו (cp. Is. xiv. 19), פגר מובס (cp. Ezek. xxiii. 44), ילוד אישה דוה (cp. Lev. xx. 18). For other names see Zunz, *Die synagogale Poesie des Mittelalters*, pp. 451 ff., and Chr. W. Christlieb, *Kurzer Auszug aus denen Selichoth oder Jüdischen Bussgebeten* (1745). It may be added that such names for Jesus are no longer to be found in modern Jewish prayer-books.

(1) *Selicha* ישראל עמך by Isaak ben Meir (12th century, *vide* Zunz, *Literaturgeschichte der synagogalen Poesie*, p. 303, Landshuth '*Ammude 'Aboda*, p. 123). Text from *Selichoth*, MS. Civit. Lips. B. H. 2 with readings from *Machzor*, Cremona, 1560, Baer's *Seder 'Abodath Jisrael* 1868, and *Selichoth*, Amsterdam, 1751.—German rite, *Selichoth le-jom sheni*.

טמאים¹ האומרים נחלתך לחבל
כבודך להמיר ואחר הבכם² להתבלבכ
נצר ונתעב³ לאלוה לקבלי⁴
ויראתך הקדושה לנטוש ולחבל⁵ :

¹ 'Ab. Jisr. טועים.   ² M. Crem. להתחבל.   ³ Sel. Amst. נצר נתעב.
⁴ 'Ab. Jisr. נטות מדרכיך ותהו לקבל.   ⁵ M. Crem., Sel. Amst. ולנבל.

(2) *Selicha* תחן אזון by an unknown author (11th or 12th cent., Zunz, l. c., p. 223, 229). Text after *Selichoth*, MS. Civit. Lips., agreeing with notices from a manuscript in *Epistolario Italiano Francese Latino di Samuel David Luzzatto*, II. (1890), p. 633, with readings from *Machzor*, Cremona, 1560, Venice, 1568 and 1715, and *Selichoth*, Amsterdam, 1751.—German rite, *Selichoth le-jom chamishi.*

שיח צגים¹ במעמד צפוף

סליחה מבקשים בקדקד כפוף

עושקיהם יקניאום בנצר נפוף²

עועים יומסכו³ ויהיו לסיפוף

פדה דביקיך מחרין וכלוי

פלטם מצורר ותנם לעילוי

צוה ישועות משחריך בחילוי

צמת בקצפך שוחחי לתלוי⁴:

¹ M. Ven. 1568 צקים. ² MS. Luzz. נאפוף, M. Ven. 1568 בנצר, M. Ven. 1568 ונתנום לשסוף. ³ M. Ven. 1568 יומשכו. ⁴ M. Crem. 1560, M. Ven. 1568 and 1715 צדקם בדינך מסתר וגלוי, Sel. Amst. צור עולמים הושיענו בגלוי.

(3) *Selicha* אודה עלי פישעי לצור by an unknown author. Text after *Selichoth*, MS. Civ. Lips., with a reading from *Machzor*, Sulzbach, 1699.—German rite, *Selichoth le-jom rebï'i she-ben Rosh ha-Shana we-Jom Kippur.*

דמינו לקאת מדבר

מת לחי¹ כחובר

והושב לי דבר

מה לתבן את הבר:

¹ M. Sulzb. פסל לאלוה.

(4) *Selicha* אליך אקרא איום by Gershom ben Jehuda (11th cent., Zunz, l. c. p. 239, Landshuth, l. c. p. 55). Text from *Selichoth*, MS. Civ. Lips., with reading from *Machzor*, Sulzbach, 1699.—German rite, *Selichoth le-jom chamishi.*

טמא ומת חדש הבא בקרוב
טבו מה אצלו ערובתו[1] לערב
יוצר הכל אייחד לקוראיו באמת קרוב
יתום ואלמנה יעודד ואביו יזרוב :
[1] M. Sulzb. אצלי ערבתי.

(5) *Selicha* אלהים אל דמי אל by an unknown author. Text from *Machzor*, Sulzbach, 1699. *Selichoth le-jom chamishi she-ben R. h. S. we-J. K.*

סמלי הקנאה וגילולימו
סחובים ילוד ואמו
סורו טמא קראו למו :

(6) *Selicha* תא שמע by Ephraim ben Jacob ben Kalonymos (12th cent., Zunz, l. c. p. 292, Landshuth, l. c. p. 47). Text from *Selichoth*, MS. Civ. Lips., with readings from *Machzor*, Cremona, 1560, from פ only after the last named source.—German rite, *Selichoth le-jom chamishi she-ben R. h. S. we-J. Kippur.*

טרו ושקלו כל יומא בי[1] ואמרין אמירא
יאי ליך עניותא כוורדא סמקא לסוסיא חיוורא
כמה גמולה את מבעליך מתכלא ועקרא
ליכי דין מיניה גט פיטורא
מתקצת מחמת מיאוס[2] ומחמת איסורא
מפסלת[3] בפיגול ונותר ונשפך הדם בעזרה
נגר בר נגר לית דפרקינך למיישרא[4]
סחיין מפיקנך[5] אלהותך מאונין הלא[6] למידכרא
ענינא רחמנא ליצלן מהאי דעתא דעבודה זרה
פתחין הבו דלא לוסיף עלה מנה למנגמרא
צוחין איברר לך אלהין ואמרינן יש ברירא
קבלת אמנתיכו לא שמיע לי דלא סבירא
רשע דקארי ליה מאי דקארי ליה בשקרא
שבועה דלא נשבקיניה עד דבילא בתרא
תקיפא הדרן עלך והדרך עלן דלא למכפרא :

[1] M. Crem. בי כל יומא. [2] M. Crem. מאוסא. [3] M. Crem. מתפסלת.
[4] M. Crem. דיפרקינך למישרא. [5] M. Crem. מפיקנא. [6] M. Crem. מאונך דלא.

(7) *Selicha* הגוים אפס ותהו probably by Kalonymos from Lucca (11th cent., Zunz, l. c. p. 108). Text from *Machzor*, MS. Civ. Lips. B. H. 3 with readings from *Machzor*, MS. Univ. Lips. 3005 and *Machzor*, Venice, 1715.—German rite, *Shacharith le-Jom Kippur.*

הגוים מכנים קדושתך לעול זימה[1]

נשואיך משקצים ייחום אשת הזימה[2]

הגוים סמל תמונת נאלה מאליהים

עמך מעידים אדונותך אלהי האלהים

הגוים פגר מובס פחזות תבליתם

צבאיך אתה קדוש יושב תהילתם:

[1] MS. Univ. Lips. הזימה.   [2] M. Ven. ערוה וזמה.

(8) *Selicha* אל ימעט לפניך by Moses ben Samuel ben Absalom (12th cent., Zunz, l. c. p. 263; Landshuth, l. c. p. 260). Text from *Selichoth*, MS. Civ. Lips. with readings from *Machzor*, Sulzbach, 1699, and *Selichoth*, Amsterdam, 1751.—German rite, *Selichoth le-Minchath Jom Kippur.*

פזר חרונך על מקניאך[1] בקנאה

פגר מת[2] משתפים לנאה גאה[3]:

[1] Sel. Amst. אויבך.   [2] M. Sulzb. פגר, Sel. Amst. מי יכול.   [3] M. Sulzb. לגואה גואה.

(9) *Selicha* אלהים אל דמי לדמי by David ben Meshullam (perhaps 12th cent., Zunz, l. c. p. 254, but cp. p. 510; Landshuth, l. c. p. 59). Text from *Selichoth*, MS. Civ. Lips. with readings from *Machzor*, MS. Civ. Lips. B. H. 3, and Sulzbach, 1699; Amsterdam, 1736.—German rite, *Selichoth le-ʿereb Rosh ha-Shana we-Jom Kippur.*

התיעצו יחד סוך[1] מסך רעל

הלוט הלוט על[2] פני כל הארץ להעל

ולא יזכר שם ישראל[3] המועל

[1] M. Sulzb. סוד.   [2] M. Civ. Lips. om. על.   [3] M. Sulzb. קדש.

ולכת אחרי התוהו מותעב⁴ ומוגעל

טף ונשים השלימו יחד⁵ לעקד

טלאים המבֻקרים בלשכת בית המוקד

יחיד ונשא עליך⁶ נהרג ונשקד⁷

ייחום הזימה⁸ אליו ראש מלייקד⁹:

⁴ M. Sulzb. מִשׁוּקַץ.   ⁵ M. Sulzb. יחד השלימו.   ⁶ M. Amst. עָלָיו.
⁷ M. Civ. Lips. וניסקד.   ⁸ M. Sulzb. יחודו נֵחַד.   ⁹ M. Sulzb. לו לבד
ראש בלי ליקוד, M. Amst. ראש לייקד.

(10) *Selicha* איה כל נפלאותיך by Gershom ben Jehuda (11th cent., Zunz, l. c. p. 239; Landshuth, l. c. p. 57). Text from *Selichoth*, MS. Civ. Lips. with readings from *Machzor*, Venice, 1568; Sulzbach, 1699; *Selichoth*, Amsterdam, 1751; Fürth, 1755.—German rite, *Selichoth le-jom shelishi*:

סגולתך דוחק צורר הצר¹

סברה להמיר² ככלי³ נוצר³:

¹ M. Sulzb. נדחק בגלות המר, Sel. Fürth דוחקת פקודתך מלנצור.
² Sel. Amst. עכום, Zunz, *Synagogale Poesie*, p. 452, תלוי, M. Ven. באמנת,
M. Sulzb. כבודך.   ³ M. Sulzb. בעת צר, Sel. Fürth סברם למצותיך
תמיד נוצר.

(11) *Zulath* אין כמוך באלמים by Isaak ben Shalom (12th cent., Zunz, l. c. p. 458; Landshuth, l. c. p. 127). Text after *Machzor*, Amsterdam, 1681, with reading from *Seder Tephilloth*, Sulzbach, 1797.—Polish rite, *first Sabbath after Pesach*.

דורשי אובות ואלילים—יאמרו אויבינו פלילים—

מה היהודים האמללים

הבו לכם עצה—פן תהיו לשמצה—הן לריב ומצה

אם תהיו כמנו—לנצר נתעב¹ תפנו—לעם אחד והיינו:

¹ Teph. Sulzb. לאובות וידעונים.

(12) *Baqqasha* אל אלהי הרוחות by Isaak Tarphan (14th or 15th cent., Zunz, l. c. p. 558; Landshuth, l. c. p. 128). Text from *Qobez Wikkuchim*, s. l. et a. (Breslau, 1844).—Not to be found in the Liturgy of the Synagogue.

יעצו כהני הבמות–להדיח את כל האומות

לעמוד ולהתפלל בין העצמות–בין[1] המרצח הזה

כל אחד ואחד יניח–ושקר וכזב יפיח

יכנה לנו שם ויביע–הכלב המת הזה[2]

למה הרגתם לעני ורש–ומבית מנוחתו נגרש

וגם דמו הנה נדרש–אבל כבד זה

מידכם ננקום נקמה–בינינו וביניכם מלחמה

כי על כל פה שומה–אם יכופר העון הזה

נגד יי ונגד משיחו–השם בשר זרועו וכחו

יחרם כחרם יריחו–אשר יאמר כי הוא זה

סומכים על קנה רצוץ–שאכל ושתה ויצא לחוץ

העצב הזה נבזה נפוץ–הרגו את האיש הזה

עצבו את איש בליעל–ולמדו מדרכי ירובעל

האתם תריבון לבעל–מה המעשה הזה

פושע מבטן כלו–לא הראנו כבודו וגדלו

יתום היה ואין עוזר לו–מדוע עשיתם הדבר הזה[3]

צבאות ישראל נצטוו בסיני–לא יבא כזה בקהל יי

הנה הוא כתוב לפני–כתבו את האיש הזה[4]

קוראים לאבן דומה–אשר אין לה תקומה

נמשל כבהמה–ויצא העגל הזה[5]

ראה כי ילוד אשה–אשר הוא מכוסה בושה

ועתה נפשנו יבשה–מה יושיענו זה[6]:

---

[1] leg. בן 2 Reg. vi. 32.   [2] 2 Sam. xvi. 9.   [3] Ex. i. 18.   [4] Jerem. xxii. 30.   [5] Ex. xxxii. 24.   [6] 1 Sam. x. 27.

(13) *Qina* זאבי ערב by Zerachja ha-Levi Gerundi (12th cent., Zunz, l. c. p. 461; Landshuth, l. c. p. 63). Text from *Seder chamesh Ta'anijjoth*, Livorno, 1877.—Spanish rite, *Shacharith le-tish'a be-Ab*.

ראשי מים לבכות ולספוד—למקדש מורש קאת וקפוד—
ומה לי לספוד לבכי ולרפוד—בראות תרפים תחת אפוד
וננע נראה בשתי וערב—בבית הארון ולוחות חורב:

(14) *Selicha* אני אני המדבר by Ephraim ben Isaac (12th
cent., Zunz, l. c. p. 278; Landshuth, l. c. p. 48). Text from
Selichoth, MS. Civ. Lips., with readings from *Machzor*, Cremona,
1560; Venice, 1715; Amsterdam, 1736.—German rite, *Selichoth
le-Musaph Jom Kippur.*

נפוגינו[1] עוצרים—כרמינו[2] בוצרים—ביום קראו נוצרים[3]
למען ספות הרווה
סבבוני בחבלם[4]—להדיחי בהבלם[5]—לנשוא סיבלם[6]—
בילוד[7] אשה דווה[8]:

[1] M. Crem. Ven. Amst. נגפונו.   [2] M. Amst. בדמינו.   [3] M. Ven.
זרים.   [4] M. Crem. בהיכלם, M. Ven. בהבלם.   [5] M. Ven. לעמלם.
[6] M. Crem. Ven. Amst. את סבלם.   [7] M. Amst. מעשה ילוד.   [8] M. Ven.
אני אנא אני בא.

(15) *Zulath* אל אל חי ארנן by Simeon ben Isaac ben Abun
(10th cent., Zunz, l. c. p. 114). Text from *Machzor*, Amsterdam,
1681, with readings from *Seder 'Abodath Jisrael*, and *Seder
Tephilloth*, Sulzbach, 1797.—Polish rite, *second Sabbath after
Pesach.*

הונוני מוני[1] בתלאה
ותנפוני ברבת חלאה
ואמרו הנה מתלאה
ומה לכם להעלב
על עסקי עון צלב[2]
נשכחתם כמת מלב:

[1] Teph. Sulzb. ישמעאל.   [2] 'Ab. Jisr. תער ונגלב בחדודי, Teph. Sulzb.
על אכילת הלב.

(16) *Zulath* אלהים לא אדע by Ephraim ben Isaac (12th cent.,
Zunz, l. c. p. 276; Landshuth, l. c. p. 48). Text from *Machzor*,

28*

Amsterdam, 1681.   Baer has in *Seder 'Abodath Jisrael* בעבור השלום "for peace's sake" quite another text.—Polish rite, *fifth Sabbath after Pesach.*

זדים עורכים לך דמות
כטעם בריר חלמות
חכמות נבל ימות
חי רוכב על עב קל
המירו באיש נסקל
ולא פנים קלקל:

ADDITIONAL NOTES.

P. 3* ix.   Add "*pal. Schabbath* 13ᵈ."
P. 3* and 11* xi.   Read "Berakhoth 17 a."
P. 18* xxiii.   For other readings see Targum Rishon to Esth. v. 9, ed. Venice, 1518, Targum Sheni to Esther iii. 1 in the same edition and p. 39* of this work.

TRANSLATIONS OF THE FOREGOING TEXTS.

I. BEN STADA, BEN PANDĒRA, PAPPOS BEN JEHUDA,
MIRJAM, THE WOMEN'S HAIRDRESSER.

(*a*)   Shabbath 104 b.   For translation, see Laible, pp. 46, and 8.

(*b*)   Sanhedrin 67 a.

"And for all capital criminals who are mentioned in the Law they do not lay an ambush but (they do) for this (criminal)." How do they act towards him?   They light the lamp for him in the innermost part of the house and they place witnesses for him in the exterior part of the house, that they may see him and hear his voice, though he cannot see them.   And that man says to him: Tell me what you have told me when we were alone.   And when he repeats (those words) to him, that man says to him: How can we abandon our God in Heaven and practise idolatry?   If he returns, it is well; but when he says: Such is our duty, and so we like to have it, then the witnesses, who are listening without, bring him to the tribunal and stone him.   And thus they have done to the Son of Stada at Lud and they hanged him on the day before Passover.

(For the rest see the translation of Shabbath 104 b.)

II. Caricature of Εὐαγγέλιον.

Shabbath 116 a. See Laible, p. 13.

Rabbi Meïr[1] calls it, "'Awen gillājōn" (blank paper, lit. margin, of evil), Rabbi Jochanan calls it, "'Awōn gillājōn" (blank paper of sin).

גליון is *margin*, paper which is left unwritten, and therefore *blank*. The Rabbis seem to have thought it remarkable that the name of the Εὐαγγέλιον did not indicate a book (ספר), but an unwritten page.

Note. These words do not stand in the Talmud in their proper place, but are a gloss to the words הגליון וספרי מינין[2] on the same page, 18 lines from the bottom.

III. The wife of Pappos ben Jehuda.

Gittin 90 a. For translation of the first part see Laible, p. 26.

And there is another who, when a fly falls into his tumbler, throws it out and drinks it, and this is the way of men generally. When she is speaking with her brothers and relatives, he does not hinder her. But there is also the man, who, when a fly falls into a dish, sucks it (the fly) out and eats it (the dish). This is the manner of a bad man, who sees his wife going out bareheaded and spinning in the street and wearing clothes slit up on both sides and bathing together with men.

(For translation of the words of Rashi, see Laible, p. 27.)

IV. A legend of Mary, and a Proverb.

(*a*) Chagiga 4 b.

When Rab Joseph came to this verse (Prov. xiii. 23) "But there is that is destroyed without judgment," he wept. He said:

---

[1] Munich MS. has דרבי מאיר קרו ליה.

[2] This is the reading of the Munich MS.

Is there really somebody who is going (away), when it is not his time? Certainly, (for) so has it happened with Rab Bibi bar Abbai, the angel of death was found with him.

(For the rest of the translation see Laible, p. 27 seq.)

(*b*) Tosaphoth Chagiga 4 b (after 'En Ja'aqob, ed. Ven. 1546).

הוה שכיח גביה מלאך המות דמספר מה שאירע לו כבר דהאי עובדא
דמרים מגדלא נשיא בבית שני היה דהיתה אמו של ישו כדאיתא בשבת:

"The angel of death was found with him," who related what had happened to him long ago, for this story as to Mirjam, the women's hairdresser, took place in the time of the second temple, for she was the mother of Jesus, as it is related in (treatise) Shabbath.

(*c*) Tosaphoth Shabbath 104 b.

"The Son of Stada." Rabbenu Tam says, that this is not Jesus the Nazarene, for as to the Son of Stada we say here that he was in the days of Pappos ben Jehuda, who lived in the days of Rabbi Aqiba, as is proved in the last chapter of Berakhoth (61 b), but Jesus lived in the days of Jehoshua ben Perachja, as is proved in the last chapter of Sota (47 a): "And not like Rabbi Jehoshua ben Perachja, who pushed away Jesus the Nazarene with both hands," and Rabbi Jehoshua was long before Rabbi Aqiba. "His mother was Mirjam, the women's hairdresser," and what is related in the first chapter of Chagiga (4 b): "Rab Bibi—the angel of death was found with him etc., he said to his messenger: Go and fetch me Mirjam, the women's hairdresser," that means that there lived in the days of Rab Bibi a Mirjam a women's hairdresser. It was another (Mirjam), or the angel of Death was also relating to Rab Bibi a story which had happened a long time before.

32*

(d) Sanhedrin 106 a (after edit. Constant. 1585).

ואת בלעם בן בעור הקוסם קוסם נביא הוא אמר רבי יוחנן בתחילה
נביא ולבסוף קוסם אמר רב פפא היינו דאמרי אינשי מסגני ושילטי הואי
איזן לגברי נגרי¹:

"And Balaam, the Son of Beor, the soothsayer" (Josh. xiii.
22). Soothsayer? he was a prophet. Rabbi Jochanan said: At
first a prophet, at last a soothsayer. Rab Papa said: This is
what people say: She was of prominent men and princes, (and
then) she prostituted herself for mere carpenters.

V. Mirjam, daughter of Bilga.

Pal. Sukka 55 d. (See Laible, p. 20.)

Bilga always receives his part on the south side on account
of Mirjam, daughter of Bilga, who turned apostate and went to
marry a soldier belonging to the government of the house of
Javan [Greece], and went and beat upon the roof of the altar.
She said to it: Wolf, wolf, thou hast destroyed the property of
the Israelites and didst not help them in the hour of their
distress!

VI. The document of Jerusalem.

Jebamoth 49 a, Mishna iv. 13.
For translation see Laible p. 31.

VII. The confession of Mary.

Kalla 18 b (41 c ed. Ven. 1528).
See Laible, pp. 33 seq.

VIII. Jesus and Jehoshua ben Perachja.

(a) Sanhedrin 107 b.
See Laible, p. 41.

¹ M in margin אזלא הויא לגבר נגרי. Rashi has also the reading נגרי.

(*b*)   Sota 47 a.

The text is substantially the same as Sanhedrin 107 b (see Laible, p. 41), therefore no special translation is necessary.

(*c*)   Pal. Chagiga 77 d.

The inhabitants of Jerusalem intended to appoint Jehuda ben Tabai as "Nasi[1]" in Jerusalem.   He fled and went away to Alexandria, and the inhabitants of Jerusalem wrote: "From Jerusalem the great to Alexandria the small.   How long lives my betrothed with you, whilst I am sitting grieved on account of him?"   When he withdrew to go in a ship, he said: Has Debora, the landlady, who has taken us in, been wanting in something?   One of his disciples said: Rabbi, her eye was bright (*i. e.* a euphemism for *blind*)!   He answered him: Lo, you have done two things; firstly, you have rendered me suspected, and then you have looked upon her.   What did I say? beautiful in appearance?   I did not say anything (like this) but (beautiful) in deeds.   And he was angry with him, and he went his way.

IX.   JESUS, THE SORCERER.

(*a*)   Shabbath 104 b.   See No. I (*a*).

(*b*)   Tosephta Shabbath XII. vers. fin.   See Laible, p. 46.

(*c*)   Pal. Shabbath 13 d.   See Laible, ibid.

He who scratches on the skin in the fashion of writing, is guilty, but he who makes marks on the skin in the fashion of writing is exempt from punishment.   Rabbi Eli'ezer said to them: But has not the Son of Stada brought (magic) spells from Egypt just in this way?   They answered him: On account of one fool we do not ruin a multitude of reasonable men.

X.   THE TESTIMONY OF JESUS AS TO HIMSELF.

(*a*)   Pal. Ta'anith 65 b.

See Laible, p. 50.

[1] President of Sanhedrin.

(*b*) Jalqut Shim'oni on Numb. xxiii. 7, under the name of Midrash Jelammedenu.

"He that blesseth his friend with a loud voice" (Prov. xxvii. 14). How strong was the voice of Balaam? Rabbi Jochanan said: (It was heard) sixty miles. Rabbi Jehoshua' ben Levi said: Seventy nations heard the voice of Balaam. Rabbi Ele-'azar ha-qappar says: God gave strength to his voice, and he went up from one end of the world to the other, because he was looking about and seeing the nations adoring the sun and the moon and the stars and wood and stone. And he looked about and saw that a man, son of a woman, will arise, who seeks to make himself God and to seduce all the world without exception. Therefore, he gave strength to his voice, that all nations of the world might hear (it), and thus he spake: Take heed that you go not astray after that man, as it is written (Num. xxiii. 19) "God is not a man, that he should lie,"—and if he says that he is God, he is a liar; and he will fall into error and say that he is going away and will come (again) at certain spaces of time, (then) he hath said and will not do it. Look what is written (Num. xxiv. 23) "And he took up his parable and said, Alas, who shall live when he makes (himself) God!" Balaam intended to say: Alas, who shall live from that nation which gives ear to that man who makes himself God?

(*c*) Pesiqta Rabbathi 100 b.

See Laible, p. 50 seq.

XI. JESUS AN IDOLATER.

(*a*) Sanhedrin 103 a. See Laible, p. 51.

"There shall no evil befall thee," Ps. xci. 10. (That means,) that evil dreams and bad phantasies shall not vex thee. "Neither shall any plague come nigh thy tent," (that means,) that thou shalt not have a son or disciple who burns his food publicly (*i.e.* who renounces openly what he has learned) like Jesus the Nazarene.

(*b*) Berakhoth 17 a seq.

When our wise men left the house of Rab Chisda or, as
others say, the house of Rab Shemuel bar Nachmani, they said
of him : " Thus our learned men[1] are laden" (Ps. cxliv. 14).
Rab and Shemuel, or, as others say, Rabbi Jochanan and Rabbi
Ele'azar (were of a different opinion). One said : "our learned"
in the Law, and " are laden" with commandments (*i.e.* good
works), and the other said : " our learned" in the Law and in
the commandments, and "are laden" with sufferings. " There
is no breaking in," that our company shall not be like the company of Saul, from whom Doeg, the Edomite, has gone out,
"and no going forth," that our company shall not be like the
company of David, from whom Ahithophel has gone out, "and
no outcry," that our company shall not be like the company of
Elisha, from whom Gehazi has gone out, "in our streets," that
we shall not have a son or disciple who burns his food publicly
like the Nazarene.

XII. BALAAM-JESUS.

(*a*) Sanhedrin XI. 90 a, Mishna x. 2.

Laible, pp. 53 seq.

(a) Sanhedrin XI. 90 a, Mishna x. 1.

Laible, pp. 55.

(β) Sanhedrin 100 b.

Laible, p. 55.

(*b*) Aboth v. 19.

Laible, p. 58.

(*c*) Sanhedrin 106 b.

Laible, p. 59.

(*d*) Sanhedrin 106 b (end).

Laible, p. 59.

[1] אלופינו, from אלף, to learn.

S.   *d*

(*e*) Sanhedrin 106 a. Laible, p. 61 seq.

"Woe to him who lives because he takes God" (Num. xxiv. 23). Resh Laqish said: Woe to him, who vivifies himself (or, who saves his life[1]) by the name of God.

Rashi.

"Balaam, who vivifies himself by the name of God," making himself God. Another reading has it: "who vivifies himself as to the name of God," that is, woe to those men that vivify and amuse themselves in this world and tear the yoke of the law from their neck and make themselves fat (משמנין).

XIII. R. Eli'ezer and Ja'aqob of Kephar Sekhanja

(*a*) 'Aboda zara 16 b seq.

Laible, pp. 62 seq.

(*b*) Qoheleth rabba to Eccles. i. 8 (Pesaro, 1519).

It is related of Rabbi Eli'ezer that he was seized for heresy. A certain governor took him and brought him up to the place of judgment to judge him. He said to him: Rabbi, shall a great man like you be occupied with such vain things? He answered: The judge is faithful towards me! and as he (the governor) imagined that he was speaking (so) on account of him, though he had only spoken in reference to Heaven (God), he said to him: Because I am faithful in your eyes, I also venture to say: Can it be that these academies are erring (and occupy themselves) with those vain things? *Dimus* (= dimissus es), you are set free. When Rabbi Eli'ezer had been dismissed from the tribunal, he was pained because he had been seized for heresy[2]. His disciples came to see him in order to comfort him, but he did not accept (their consolation). (Then) Rabbi Aqiba came to see him and said to him: Rabbi, perhaps one of the heretics has said before you some word which pleased you. He answered: Lo, by Heaven, you remind me. Once, when I was going up

[1] Comp. *Midrash Tanchuma*, *Mattoth*, ed. Mantua 1563, fol. 91 c.

[2] על דברי מינות is a gloss.

in the street of Zippori, a man, named Ja'aqob of Kephar Sekhanja, came to me and told me something from Jesus, son of Pandēra, and I liked it. And this it was: It is written in your Law (Deut. xxiii. 18); "Thou shalt not bring the hire of a whore or the wages of a dog (into the House of Jahve):" how is it with them? I said: They are forbidden. He said to me: Forbidden for sacrifice, but allowed for purposes of destruction. I said to him: But what may then be done with them? He answered: You may build with them baths and privies. I said to him: You have said well, for at this time the Halakha was hidden from me. When he saw that I praised his words, he said to me: Thus the Son of Pandēra hath said: from filth they went, to filth they may go, as it is said (Mic. i. 7): "for of the hire of an harlot she gathered them, and unto the hire of an harlot shall they return;" they may be applied to public privies. This pleased me, and, therefore, I have been seized for heresy, and also because I transgressed what is written in the Law (Prov. v. 8): "Remove thy way far from her"—that is the heresy.

XIV. Imma Shalom, Rabban Gamliel and the "Philosopher."

Shabbath 116 a seq.

Laible, pp. 66 seq.

XV. The five disciples of Jesus.

Sanhedrin 43 a.

Laible, pp. 85 seq. and 71 seq.

XVI. Ja'aqob of Kephar Sekhanja, the performer of miracles.

(*a*)   Pal. Shabbath 14 d (lower part).

Laible, p. 77.

(*b*)   Bab. 'Aboda zara 27 b.

Laible, p. 78.

XVII. Another Christian who performs miracles.

(*a*) Pal. 'Aboda zara 40 d. Laible, p. 77 seq.

His grandson (the grandson of Jehoshua' ben Levi) had swallowed something. A man came and whispered to him (a spell) in the name of Jesus son of Pandēra and he got well. When he went out, he (Jehoshua' ben Levi) asked him: What did you say over him (read עלוי)? He answered: According to the word of somebody. He said: What had been his fate, had he died and not heard this word? And it happened to him, "as it were an error which proceedeth from the ruler" (Eccles. x. 5).

(*b*) Qoheleth rabba to Eccles. x. 5.

The son of Rabbi Jehoshua' ben Levi had something in his throat. He went and fetched one of the men of the son of Pandēra, to bring out what he had swallowed. He (Jehoshua' ben Levi) said to him: What didst thou say over him? He answered: A certain verse after a certain man (?). He said: It had been better for him, had he buried him and not said over him that verse. And so it happened to him, "as it were an error which proceedeth from the ruler" (Eccles. x. 5).

XVIII. The condemnation of Jesus.

(*a*) Sanhedrin 67 a (see I. above).

(*b*) Pal. Sanhedrin 25 c seq. Laible, p. 79 seq.

XIX. The execution of Jesus.

Sanhedrin 43 a (see above, No. XV.).

XX. The Academy of the Son of Pandēra.

Targum Sheni to Esther vii. 9.

Laible, p. 90.

XXI. Jesus in Hell.

(*a*) Gittin 56 b seq.

Laible, pp. 92 seq.

(*b*) Tosaphoth to 'Erubin 21 b.

"Is there (Eccles. xii. 12) then really written לַעַג (derision)?"
At all events[1] it is true that he is punished by boiling filth,
as we are saying in Ha-Nezaqin (Chapter v. of treatise Gittin,
fol. 56 b).

XXII. Mirjam, daughter of Eli, in Hell.

Pal. Chagiga 77 d.

Laible, p. 30.

XXIII. The ancestors of Haman.

Sopherim xiii. 6 ; various readings from Targum I to Esther
v. 1 (Ven. 1518) and from Targum II to Esther iii. 1 (Ven. 1518).

בתר פתגמיא האילין רבי מלכא אחשורוש ית המן בן¹ המדתא אגגא²
בר כוזא³ בר ²פוליטוס⁴ בר דיוס⁵ בר דיוסוס⁶ בר פרוס⁷ בר נידן⁸ בר
בעלקן⁹ בר אוטימרוס¹⁰ בר הדום¹¹ בר הדורוס¹² בר שנר בר נגר בר
פרמישתא בר ויזתא¹³ בר עמלק בר לחינתיה דאליפז¹⁴ בוכריה דעשו¹⁵ :

¹ Targ. I בר.   ² Targ. I בר עדא, Targ. II בר סרח.אגניא בר סרח   ³ Targ. I
ביזנאי, Targ. II בוזה.   ⁴ Targ I אפליטוס, Targ. II איפלוטוס.
⁵ Targ. I om.   ⁶ Targ. II דיוסים.   ⁷ Targ. I פירוס, Targ. II פדום.
⁸ Targ. I המדן, Targ. II מעדן.   ⁹ Targ. I תליון, Targ. II בלעקן.
¹⁰ Targ. I אתנימסוס, Targ. II אנתימרוס.   ¹¹ Targ. I חרום, Targ. II
om.   ¹² Targ. I חרסום, Targ. II הדירום.   ¹³ Targ. I add
בר אגג בר סומקר.   ¹⁴ Targ. I בר אליפז.   ¹⁵ Targ. I בר עשו רשיעא.

After these events King Achashwerosh made great Haman,
the son of Hammedatha, the Agagite, son of Kuza (comp.
Χουζᾶς, Luk. viii. 3), son of Apolitos (comp. Πλοῦτος), son of

---

[1] The Tosaphoth mean, although it may not be allowed to derive this
manner of punishment from the words in Eccles. xii. 12, as Rab Acha bar
Ulla does, 'Erubin 21 b, it is nevertheless true.

Dios (comp. Διός, gen. of Ζεύς), son of Diosos (comp. Διόνυσος)
son of Paros (comp. Varus), son of Nedan (comp. Νήρων), son
of Beʿelqan (?), son of Otimeros (?), son of Hados (comp. Ἄδης),
son of Hadoros (comp. Ἡρώδης, Taʿan. 23 a הורודוס), son of Sheger
(a young calf, comp. שגר, Exod. xiii. 12 and Targ. Onk.), son of
Naggar (a carpenter), son of Parmashta (comp. Esth. ix. 9), son
of Vajzatha (comp. Esth. ix. 9), son of ʿAmaleq, son of the con-
cubine of Eliphaz, the firstborn of ʿEsau.

XXIV. JESUS IN THE ZOHAR.

Zohar III. 282 a (Rāʿjā mehēmnā).

From the side of idolatry Shabbethaj (Saturn) is called Lilith[1],
mixed dung, on account of the filth mixed from all kinds of dirt
and worms, into which they throw dead dogs and dead asses,
the sons of ʿEsau and Ishmaʿel, and there (read ובה) Jesus and
Mohammed, who are dead dogs, are buried among them. She
(Lilith) is the grave of idolatry, where they bury the uncir-
cumcised, (who are) dead dogs, abomination and bad smell, soiled
and fetid, a bad family. She (Lilith) is the ligament[2] which
holds fast the "mixed multitude" (Ex. xii. 38), which is mixed
among Israel, and which holds fast bone and flesh, that is, the
sons of ʿEsau and Ishmaʿel, dead bone and unclean flesh torn
of beasts in the field, of which it is said (Ex. xxii. 31): "Ye
shall cast it to the dogs."

XXV. JESUS IN THE LITURGY OF THE SYNAGOGUE.

1. Selicha ישראל עמך.

Unclean are they who mean to spoil thy inheritance,
> that it may barter away thy glory and become entangled
> > after their vanity,
> to accept the "abominable branch" (Is. xiv. 19) as God,
> and to cast away and to spoil thy holy fear.

---

[1] Lilith is a female demon, comp. Is. xxxiv. 14 and Weber, *Altsynagogale
palästinische Theologie*, p. 246.

[2] סרכא is a fibre attached to the lungs.

2.   Selicha אזון תחי.

They that are raising lamentation in a depressed condition,
   asking forgiveness with a head bowed down,
Their oppressors make them angry by the branch of adultery.
   With perverseness may they be mingled (Is. xix. 14) and be
      left to destruction,
Deliver thy adherents from doom and consumption (Is. x. 23),
   let them escape from the oppressor and make them the
      highest (Deut. xxvi. 19).
Command the salvation of those that search thee with appeasing,
   destroy in thy wrath those that bow to a hanged one!

3.   Selicha אודה על פשעי לצור.

We are like the pelican of the wilderness (Ps. cii. 6),
   as though a dead man were joined to a living one[1] (Eccles.
      ix. 5),
And it is answered to me,
   What is the straw to the wheat (Jer. xxiii. 28)?

4.   Selicha אליך אקרא איום.

An unclean and dead man, a new comer from nigh at hand,
   what is his person to me (אצלי) that I should become surety
      for him (Prov. xvii. 18)?
I will praise the unity of him who formed the universe, nigh to
      them who call upon him in truth,
   the fatherless and the widow he upholdeth (Ps. cxlvi. 9), but
      he pulls down[2] his enemies.

[1] Our position is quite as unnatural as the conjunction of a dead and a living man would be. This *may be* an allusion to our Christian belief in the Crucified who is the Son of the living God or to the idolatry of the Romish Church, but it is not *necessarily* so.

[2] See Job vi. 17 and comp. the Targum.

5. Selicha אלהים אל דמי אל.

The images of jealousy (Ez. viii. 3) and their idols,
> they are dragged, the child and his mother ;
> depart ye, unclean. they (the Jews) cry unto them (Lament.
> iv. 15).

6. Selicha תא שמע.

They dispute with me all the day and hold their talk.

Poverty fits thee as a red rose to a white horse (Chag. 9 b).

How greatly art thou weaned from thy husband, who art
> bereaved of children and barren,

Here is for thee from him the letter of divorce (Gitt. ix. 3) !

Thou hast been declared separated (מוקצה) because of offensive-
> ness and because of prohibition (Shabb. 44 a),

Thou hast been declared illicit (פסול) by pronouncing thee "an
> abomination" and "remainder" (Lev. xix. 6, 7) and
> (an offering) the blood (of which) has been shed on
> the court (Zebach. ii. 1)[1],

There is no carpenter, son of a carpenter, who could release thee
> (Ab. zar. 50 b) in order to declare (thee) allowed[2].

They say : We shall remove thy deity from thy ear (Jeb. 60 b),
> (so as) not to (דלא) remember it.

We answer : The Merciful One save us from such an idolatrous
> thought (Shabb. 84 b) !

They begin : Come on, (so as) not to continue with it, in order to
> learn from it[3],

---

[1] Both this verse and the preceding one begin with מ. Probably the
first of the two is spurious and a gloss to the second.—The remainder of a
peace-offering may not be eaten and is פגול ; likewise an offer is illicit
when its blood has been shed into the court instead of being brought to the
altar. *Perhaps* the last words are an allusion to the killing of Zachariah
in the Temple (2 Chron. xxiv. 20, Matt. xxiii. 35, Gitt. 57 b) and further
to the crucifixion of Christ.

[2] No wise man exists who can remove all objections and declare thee
allowed, that is, nobody can put an end to thy repudiation by God.· An
allusion to Jesus, the carpenter, is not intended.

[3] The law of Moses shall be left.

They cry: I will select Gods for thee, but we say: There is
(already) a selection (Bekh. 57 a),

The tradition of your faith I do not hear nor understand
(ולא סבירא),

(Him), the wicked one whom they call as they call him by fraud[1].

We swear that we shall not forsake Him till the last shovel
(Ber. 8 a)[2],

Almighty one, we return to thee and thou returnest to us[3],
never to be denied.

7.   Rahit הגוים אפס ותהו.

The nations impute thy holy name to a child of lewdness,
They that are borne by thee make to be abominable the
offspring of the lust of a lewd woman (Ez. xxiii. 44).

The nations deify the idol of the image of a corrupt man (read
נאלח and comp. Job xv. 16),
Thy people bear witness to thy supremacy, thou, God of
Gods,

The nations—a carcase trodden under foot (Is. xiv. 19) is the
wantonness of their impudicity (Is. x. 25 and Targum),
Thy hosts—thou art the holy one, inhabiting their praise
(Ps. xxii. 4).

8.   Selicha אל ימעט לפניך.

Scatter thy wrath on them who make thee jealous with jealousy,
who join a dead carcase to the Most High (Ex. xv. 1).

---

[1] Jesus is this "wicked one" who is called by a certain name (i.e. by the name of God).

[2] Till the last shovel, *i. e.* until we shall lie in our grave.

[3] This formula is written at the end of all the treatises in the Talmud. It originally refers to the treatise, not to God.

9. Selicha אלהים אל דמי לדמי.

They take counsel together to pour out the mixed wine of
    reeling,
      to lift the covering veil (Is. xxv. 7) (to spread it) over all
        the earth,
      and the exalted holy name (שם קו״ש) shall not be re-
        membered,
      and to follow the vanity which is abominable and dis-
        gusting.

    ...   .

Children and women made a covenant together to be bound
    like lambs which are examined in the chamber of the house
      of burning[1].
    Thou, the sole and exalted One, for thee we will be killed
      and pierced (comp. Lam. i. 14 and the Jewish Com-
      mentaries),
    (so as) not to bow down the head to him, the (offspring of
      the) lust of lewdness.

10. Selicha איה כל נפלאותיך.

Thy peculiar people is forced on by an adversary oppressing,
    To fix its hope in exchange on the hanged one, an idol
      (literally, who is made) (בתלוי נוצר)[2].

11. Zulath אין כמוך באלמים.

They that seek unto wizards and idols,
    our enemies and judges (Deut. xxxii. 31), say :
    What (do) these feeble Jews (Neh. iii. 34)?
Give ye your counsel (2 Sam. xvi. 20),
    that you may not be for a derision (Ex. xxxii. 25),
    behold, for strife and contention (Is. lviii. 4).

---

[1] A place in the Temple, see Tamid i. 1. In fact, however, the lambs
were not examined there, but in a chamber near to it. See Tamid iii. 3.

[2] נוצר is an allusion to נוצרי ' Nazarene.

If ye will be as we be (Gen. xxxiv. 15),
> and turn to the abominable branch (Is. xiv. 19),
> then we will become one people (Gen. xxxiv. 16).

12. Baqqasha אל אלהי הרוחות.

The priests of the high places have resolved
> to seduce all nations,
> to stand and to pray between the bones
> of this son (read בן) of a murderer (2 Kings vi. 32).

Everyone barks (in derision : read יבח)
> and breathes out falsehood and lies,
> he gives us an (insulting) nickname and pours (it) out,
> this dead dog (2 Sam. xvi. 9).

Why did you kill the miserable and poor
> and him who was driven away from his house of rest ?
> Therefore, also, behold, his blood is required (Gen. xlii. 22),
> this grievous mourning (Gen. l. 11).

On you we will take revenge,
> between us and you is war,
> for it is the resolve of all (literally, it is laid on every mouth
>> 2 Sam. xiii. 32):
> surely this iniquity shall not be purged (Is. xxii. 14) !

In the presence of the Lord and His anointed (1 Sam. xii. 3),
> he who makes flesh his arm and his strength,
> be anathematized as with the anathema of Jericho (Josh.
>> vi. 17, 26) ;
> he who says, This is he (Ex. xxii. 8).

They that rely on a bruised reed,
> (on a man) who ate and drank and went out,
> this despised broken image (Jer. xxii. 28),
> kill ye this man (Jer. xxxviii. 4) !

Leave ye (read עזבו) the man of Belial,
and learn from the ways of Jerubbaal[1].
Will ye plead for Baal (Judg. vi. 31)?
What deed is this (Gen. xliv. 15)?
He is a transgressor from the womb altogether,
he has not shewed us his glory and his greatness (Deut. v.
24);
fatherless he was and had none to help him (Job xxix. 12).
Why have ye done this thing (Ex. i. 18)?
The hosts of Israel have received commandment on Sinai,
such a one[2] shall not enter into the assembly of the Lord
(Deut. xxiii. 3),
behold, of him is written before me:
write ye this man (as childless, Jerem. xxii. 30)!
They that invoke a dumb stone (Hab. ii. 19),
which has not power to rise (Lev. xxvi. 37),
it is like a beast,
and there came out this calf (Ex. xxxii. 24).
See he is (a man,) born of a woman,
who is covered with shame,
and now, our soul is dried away (Num. xi. 6),
how shall this man save us (1 Sam. x. 27)?

13.   Qina זאבי ערב.

My head is like water for weeping and wailing
for the sanctuary that is a possession of the pelican and the
porcupine (Is. xxxiv. 11),
and how shall I wail and spread (?) for weeping,
when I see Teraphim in the place of the Ephod,
and a stain is to be seen in the warp and woof (Lev. xiii.
47, 48)[3]
in the house of the ark and the tables of Horeb.

---

[1] Jerubbaal said of Baal, whose altar he had thrown down: If he be
a god, let him plead for himself!

[2] A bastard (ממזר) like Jesus as the offspring of an illegitimate birth.

[3] "Warp and woof" is a Jewish term for the cross. The meaning is

14. Selicha אני אני המדבר.

Vexations have slain us (read נגפונו),
  cutting up our vineyards,
  when the Nazarenes call (us),
  to add moist (to dry, Deut. xxix. 18)[1].
They have surrounded me with their cord,
  to seduce me by their vanity,
  to bear their burden,
  the work (image) of a child of a woman having her sick-
    ness (Lev. xx. 18).

15. Zulath אל אל חי ארנן.

My oppressors oppress me by weariness
  and defile me by "great rust" (Ez. xxiv. 12),
  and say: Behold, what a weariness (Mal. i. 13)!
And why should ye be anxious
  about the sin of the cross?
  (or, else) ye are forgotten as a dead man out of mind (Ps.
    xxxi. 13).

16. Zulath אלהים לא אדע.

Proud men make to thee a comparison (Is. xl. 18),
  as the taste of the white of an egg (Job vi. 6),
  should he (as God) die as a fool dieth (2 Sam. iii. 33)?
The living one who rideth upon a swift cloud (Is. xix. 1)
  they have exchanged for a stoned man
  and one who did not whet the edge[2] (Eccl. x. 10).

that the cross in the place of the former temple is a profanation and defile-
ment of the holy place.

[1] Targ. Onkelos translates Deut. xxix. 18: to add the sins of error to
(the sins of) presumption. Perhaps something like this is intended by the
poet.

[2] His iron had been made blunt, and he did not whet it,—that is, he was
killed and could not restore himself to life.

JESUS CHRIST IN THE TALMUD

BY

HEINRICH LAIBLE

TRANSLATED BY

REV. A. W. STREANE.

JESUS CHRIST IN THE TALMUD.

INTRODUCTION.

IT is a fact well known, alike to Jewish and Christian students of Hebrew literature, that certain passages of the Talmud have been erased by the "censure[1]."

Nor is this merely a matter of somewhat ancient history. We cannot quite accept the plea, if adduced by Jews of the present day, that such passages contain no interest for them; that Jesus was a zākēn mamrē (a heterodox teacher; cp. e.g. *Mish. Sanh.* XI. 2), who no longer concerns them, whom they neither love nor hate.

On the other hand it is a fact, known to Jews much earlier than to Christians, that the Jewish collections of passages thus excised[2] belong to a very recent date, that they have only been printed within the last few decades and some of them in *Germany*. Accordingly the passages in the Talmud referring to our Lord are by no means unknown to the Jews of the

---

[1] The action of the "censor," as representing the secular (Christian) power. Many passages were excised in this way, under the belief that the Talmud contained attacks on Christianity. [A. W. S.].

[2] H. Strack, *Einleitung in den Thalmud*, Leipzig, 1887, p. 53, adduces four of them. In that work much is explained, which here for brevity's sake had to be presupposed as known, such as the names of the treatises which form the Talmud, the mode of citation, technical expressions, such as Boraitha, Tosephta, etc. (An enlarged and improved edition will shortly appear.)

present day; much less are they wholly unimportant in their
eyes; otherwise they surely would not have been purposely
circulated by them through the press[1]. It follows that a
treatise, which bears the title "Jesus Christ in the Talmud,"
were it only by reason of its subject, addresses itself to living
Jewish interests.

We may here be permitted to comment briefly upon a statement which appears in a recent publication. Ad. Blumenthal
in his "Open letter to Prof. Delitzsch" (Frankfort-on-the-Main,
1889, pp. 7 ff.) has alleged that the invectives against Christ,
as contained in the Talmud, have been evoked by Christian
persecutions! He transfers the later persecution of Jews to the
infancy of the Church. But the Jewish hatred of Christianity,
which began with the Crucifixion of Christ, is much older than
the Christian hatred of the Jew. It is enough to recall the
two names of St Paul and Justin[2]. Further, we may note that
Blumenthal himself declines on any one occasion to write in full
the name of Jesus, but contents himself with signifying it by
the initial letter. Again, Lippe, while denying in his pamphlet[3]
that any Jesus myths in the Talmud have to do with Jesus of
Nazareth, is yet himself capable of very intemperate language
towards the Founder of Christianity.

Our aim in this treatise is not to wound the Jews, or to
supply their enemies with a weapon. Rather it is to make good,
as far as we may, the faults which the 'censorship' of earlier time
has committed with regard to the Talmud. The Amsterdam
edition of the year 1644 is the last which contains a considerable
portion of the passages in question. Even of late, notwithstanding
that outside Russia the 'censorship' on the part of Christians
does not stand in the way, only mutilated texts of the Talmud

[1] These collections of passages excluded by the *Censure* are for the
most part intentionally printed without mention of places, and have not
been announced in the book trade.

[2] See Appendix I. for quotations from the latter. [A. W. S.]

[3] *The Gospel of St Matthew before the tribunal of the Bible and of the
Talmud*, Jassy, 18 9.

have been printed. Compare, for the 'censorship' which the Jews themselves wilfully practise with regard to the Talmud, Strack's *Einleitung (Introduction)*, p. 52. Everyone therefore who desires to see with his own eyes what the Talmud contains as to Jesus and Christianity, must either go to those libraries where there are still to be found old editions of the Talmud, or must seek to provide himself with a copy of the collection of passages omitted by the 'censure,' such as I have already referred to. It is a general wish of all Christian, and surely also of some Jewish, men of learning, who study the Talmud, that once again it should appear in a complete form. "And since," as Strack says (p. 50), "we shall still have to wait long for a critical edition of the Babylonian Talmud, the desire may be permitted, that meanwhile some amount of compensation be offered by a speedy printing of the text of the Munich Manuscript." A sample, but only just a sample, of a critically restored text is presented to us in the edition of the treatise *Makkoth* by Friedmann (Vienna, 1888). It was at bottom a thoroughly Talmudic[1] principle, which the Romish Church followed, when it gave the order, to purify the Talmud from everything hostile to Christianity. Very different was the view of the Church teacher, Origen. His words directed against the slanderous writings of Celsus (I. 1) are as follows: "Our Saviour held His peace, when He was charged before the heathen governor. He believed that the holiness and innocence of His walk would vindicate Him much more forcibly than scorn however eloquently phrased. Let us also in this matter tread in the steps of Jesus. We are abused, reviled, slandered, accused, persecuted, slain. Let us with our Redeemer keep silence, and oppose to our enemies nothing save our piety, our love, our meekness, our humility. Piety speaks without words more eloquently and powerfully

---

[1] R. Tarphon [head of the Jewish academy of Lud (see p. 38), a contemporary of Akiba, A. W. S.] said: "During the lifetime of my children, had the writings of the Christians come into my hands, I would have consumed them together with the names of God, which they contain." *Shabbath*, fol. 116 a.

than the most eloquent reasoning." Have then the burning of
the Talmud and such other violent measures as may have been
adopted against it effected what the Church must desire, viz., to
diminish the Jews' hatred of Christ, or to make them more
friendly towards Christianity? The result was the opposite of
that aimed at. The passages erased from the Talmud became so
much the dearer to the Jews. They took care that they should
be secretly propagated. What at an earlier time was scattered
through the Talmud, the Jews have now in a combined form
in the above-mentioned collections of passages omitted by the
'censure,' and there is no question that such a collocation, in
itself already adapted to carry forward the opposition more
vividly and to accentuate it more sharply, furnishes fresh nutri-
ment to the existing hatred against the Christians, inasmuch as
the Jew says to himself, "These are the important passages
from our Talmud, of which the Goyim have desired to rob us."

Against such a policy of destruction however a protest must
also be made in the name of history. It is thoroughly objection-
able, that an ancient literary work should be arbitrarily altered
or mutilated by after ages. And what a misdemeanour towards
history it is, forcibly to suppress historical facts! What the
Talmud contains concerning our Lord, even though it be for the
most part a distortion of truth or even a purely imaginary
picture, yet is history all the same, a history, that is to say, of
Jewish ideas concerning a Person of transcendent interest.

We consider therefore that in restoring to the Jews the
passages in question, we are in some sense making amends for
the acts of folly committed towards them by the Church in its
unwisdom. This is possible, notwithstanding that the Jews
have never been altogether deprived of them. For it may still
be rightly named a restitution, if we, unlike the Pope, call upon
the Jews: "Do but study just these Talmudic passages about
Christ with real thoroughness. For a thorough study of these
passages must, as we think, shake *the belief of the Jews in the
authority of the Talmud*, by their perceiving how far in all
matter concerning Jesus it has departed from the sources of

truth," and must further induce the Jews to read the New Testament, the perusal of which Prof. Delitzsch has made more attractive for them by his classical translation of it into Hebrew. Since however it is confessedly a difficulty to many a Jew to examine into the truth of the Talmud, in whose authority he comes prepared with an unconditional belief, it is now a task for Christians on their side to examine scientifically the Talmudic traditions concerning our Lord, and to point out their origin.

However, to render a service to the Jews is not the only point of view from which the subject of "Jesus Christ in the Talmud" seems deserving of a thorough investigation. Jesus is a name which has no parallel. No one passes Him by with indifference. And the question which stirs all the world, What think ye of Christ? experiences from none a more significant answer than from the people of the Promise. In unbelief, as in belief, the Jews are the leaders of mankind. And therefore it is that we also read in the Gospels, with an interest quite other than if the case concerned the heathen, how the Jews dealt with Christ. With precisely the same interest must we read the Jewish traditions about Jesus in the Talmud.

But then, although we might have cherished the expectation of finding in the huge Talmud, containing, as it does, specially religious discussions of every kind, the Person and the acts and teaching of Christ very expressly and frequently debated, the astonishing fact confronts us, that Jesus is very seldom spoken of, and but little is known of Him. The case, that is to say, is not, as was formerly believed on the part of Christians, that the Talmud abounded in abuse of Christ. This is a Christian error, which sprang probably from the belief that everything said in the Talmud in reference to idolatry and to Rome was aimed at Christians. No, in the Talmud, so far as the existing matter permits us to judge, mention of Jesus occurs but sparingly. It seems inexplicable that the scribes, who in Jesus' lifetime busied themselves with Him day and night, whose disposition also in the Talmud is still the same one of hostility, have become comparatively so silent, and that too in spite of the fact that Christianity was advancing with such rapid strides. But in the first place it must be borne in mind that the growth of the Church was ever, so to speak, developing itself less under the eyes of the Jews, and more at a distance from them. It was not where the Jews dwelt and their Academies existed, viz. in Palestine and Babylon, that the Gospel had extended itself, as a tree embracing all within its shade, but like the sun and the history of the nations of the world it made its way to the west, where by its gentle power it gained one victory after another. It is conceivable that when the occasion for combating an enemy is lacking, he may not be particularly frequently spoken of. Only once there arose an embittered strife against the Christians, namely in the time of Bar Kokh'ba, the false Messiah, and of R. Akiba, his prophet, who was a fierce enemy of Jesus (see below, p. 38). But otherwise there was peace, and so they might easily, absorbed in the study of the Law, and disturbed therein by no Christian, have altogether ignored Jesus, if it were not that He was just a Person whom the Jew cannot in the long run pass by, without crucifying Him, or else—worshipping Him. As long as the earth remains, Jesus will never be forgotten by the Jews. But what could the Jews know about Jesus? The writings of the Christians, in which there stood much concerning Him, were burnt rather than read; and oral teaching was just as little sought at the hands of Christians. What therefore out of the whole rich history of Jesus could remain over, except certain main features, which had already become indistinct, when a Rabbi gave them stereotyped expression, and which, in later time, were still less understood? Or, prompted by such traditions, people yielded to the impulse to complete them, or even delivered themselves altogether to poetic fancy, which of course introduced no *historical* features, but yet did introduce such as fitted well into the picture which they had formed of Jesus. But, as has been said, while on the side of Christianity, no considerable inducement was given to the Jews to call Jesus to mind, so the really vigorous current of Jewish life failed to concern itself much about Him. How totally different was it in the middle ages! In that period, the time of the Jewish persecutions, the hatred of Jesus, which was never quite dormant, reached its full expression, and begat a literature, in comparison with which the Talmud must be termed almost innocent. Then there was found in the very name of Jesus the treatment which He deserved, viz. to be blotted out[1], and in the *Tol'doth Jeshu* there was put together a detailed picture of the life of Jesus, of which the authors of the Talmud had no anticipation[2].

Our examination of the sayings in the Talmud falls into three main divisions: the first, and at the same time the most comprehensive, is concerned with the designations of Jesus and His origin, the second deals with Jesus' works, the third with His Death.

I. DESIGNATIONS OF JESUS AND HIS ORIGIN.

Common appellations of Jesus in the Talmud and in Talmudic literature are the expressions "Son of Stada (Satda)," and "Son of Pandēra." They are so stereotyped that they appear constantly in the Babylonian Talmud (cp. the Targum

[1] The three consonants j, s (shin), v, with which the name Jeshu was written, are explained as being the first letters of the three words *Jimmach sh'mo w'zikhro* (May his name and his memory be blotted out!). It is not certain when the Jews began to explain ישׁי by ימח שמו וזכרו. The first witness is the mediæval Tol'doth Jeshu. But the edition of this work by Joh. Jac. Huldrich (1705) has ימח זכרו וימח שמו as explanation of the name ישׁוּ "Jesus." The ritual of the Synagogue has ימח שמו וזכרו on Amalek or Edom in the liturgy for Shabbath Zakhor. See the German Machāzor, II fol. 79ᵃ, ed. of Venice 1568. It is well known that Amalek or Edom is for the mediæval Jews the representative of the Christian nations or even the Church. [G. D.]

[2] A new edition of the Tol'doth Jeshu has been edited by Gershom Bader under the title Chelkath M'chokek, 1st ed., Jerusalem, 1880; 2nd ed., Krakau without year. The editor speaks of three MSS., which he used for his edition, but confesses that he did not utilise them fully. [G. D.]

Sheni on Esth. vii. 9) without the name Jesus. It might for this reason seem to be a question who it is precisely that is to be understood thereby. But in the Jerusalem Talmud, *Aboda Zara* II. 40d, the name is *Jeshu ben Pandēra* (for which more briefly *Shabbath* XIV. 14d has *Jeshu Pandēra*); and in the Tosephta on Chullin II. near the end (ed. Zuckermandel, p. 503), *Jeshu*ᵃᶜ *ben Pantēra* and *Jeshu*ᵃᶜ *ben Pantērē*. Moreover, the Jesus who (*Sanhedrin* 43a)[1] "is hanged on the evening but one before the Passover," is on the other hand (*Sanh.* 67a)[2] called son of Stada (Satda). It is evident that in both places the same person is treated of. The passage of singular import, occurring, as it does, twice in precisely similar language, and further, in that treatise which is chiefly concerned with Jesus, proves clearly the identity of Jesus and Ben Stada (Satda).

How indiscriminate however was the use of the two titles Ben Stada (Satda) and Ben Pandēra, and not only so, but also how little clearness there was with regard to them is shewn by two remarkable and almost verbally identical passages *Shabbath* 104b[3] and *Sanhedrin* 67a,.the former of which[4] we present here in a literal translation. It runs as follows: "The son of Stada was son of Pandēra. Rab Chisda said: The husband was Stada, the lover Pandēra. (Another said), The husband was Paphos ben Jehudah; Stada was his mother; (or) his mother was Miriam, the women's hairdresser; as they would say at Pumbeditha[5], *S'tath da* (i.e. she was unfaithful) to her husband." In

----

[1] See (German) p. 15*, XIX.

[2] See do. p. 5*, I. (b).

[3] See do. p. 5*, I. (a).

[4] *Shabbath* 104b is not a discussion between Rab Chisda and other learned men, but the Gemara here collects different views. It is only the saying, "the husband was Stada, the lover Pandēra," which is with certainty to be ascribed to Rab Chasda. [G. D.]

[5] Called also Golah (captivity), as an abode of Jewish exiles, about seven miles N. of Sora; probably at the mouth (*pum*) of a canal called Beditha. It was the residence of the chief Jewish families of Babylonia, but as the seat of an academy it was later than Sora, while on the other hand its school was more permanent and of a still more influential character. The people

more intelligible language, with the needful additions, which are
so constantly lacking in the Talmud by reason of its conciseness,
the passage runs thus : "He was not the son of Stada, but he
was the son of Pandēra. Rab Chisda said : The husband of
Jesus' mother was Stada, but her lover was Pandēra. Another
said Her husband was surely Paphos ben Jehudah ; on the contrary Stada was his mother : or, according to others, his mother
was Miriam, the women's hairdresser. The rejoinder is : Quite
so, but Stada is her nickname, as it is said at Pumbeditha,
S'ṭath da (she proved faithless) to her husband."

This passage, noteworthy from every point of view, dates
from the end of the third or the beginning of the fourth century
after Christ. For R. Chisda (died A.D. 309[1]) belongs to the
third generation of the Amoraim, and lived at Sora, the Babylonian Academy founded by Rab[2]. At this late date accordingly
the question was started, which of the two familiar designations
(son of Stada, son of Pandēra) was the correct one? It was
natural that this question should some time emerge. One of the
two appellations appeared to be necessarily false. Which was
correct?

The subject treated in the preceding context was that Ben
Stada had brought charms with him out of Egypt in an incision
in his flesh. Thereupon some one objects : "The designation
Ben Stada is false ; he was the son of Pandēra." Whereupon
the opinion of Rab Chisda is at once adduced : "No ; both
names are easily possible. You know at any rate that Jesus
was illegitimate. Consequently the one name is that of his
legal, the other that of his natural father, and indeed I give as
my decision that Stada was the husband of the mother of Jesus,
while Pandēra on the other hand was the name of her paramour.

of the place had an evil reputation for theft and fraud. See further in Neubauer's *Géographie du Talmud*, p. 349. [A. W. S.]

[1] He was head of the Sora Academy A.D. 290—300. [A. W. S.]

[2] Thus called *par excellence*, as the greatest of all teachers of that period.
He was a Babylonian, and presided at Sora for twenty-four years, dying
A.D. 243. [A. W. S.]

It is accordingly right to call him indifferently a son of Stada or a son of Pandēra." But against this a different tradition is quoted. "The husband of the mother of Jesus was surely Paphos ben Jehudah. Stada on the contrary is not a man's name at all, but by it we are to understand Jesus' mother." This does not deal with the name Pandēra; but grants Rab Chasda's view, that Pandēra was the paramour of Jesus' mother. Some-one else opposes the assertion that Jesus' mother was named Stada, in the words: "But it is admitted, that the mother of Jesus was Miriam, the women's hairdresser." Thereupon follows as rejoinder to this the conclusion: "Of that we too are aware. But she is also called Stada, i.e. as her nickname. Insomuch as she had intercourse with a lover and bore him Jesus, she was given the *sobriquet* Stada, which consists of the two words *s'ṭath da*, i.e. she has been unfaithful, namely to her husband. So at least the word is explained in the Babylonian Academy at Pumbeditha."

From these passages two things are clear; first, that at that time Jesus was in truth still a most weighty name, but secondly, that there was very seldom among the Jews any discussion as to the circumstances of His life, so that, on the occasion of any question being raised as to those circumstances, great uncertainty, coupled with complete ignorance, was shewn. This would have been impossible, if at that time any intercourse had still obtained between Jesus and Christians. Both parties, as we clearly see, had long since done with one another.

1. With regard to the individual assertions set forth in the passages, we must in the next place examine an historical remark as well as an etymological explanation. We begin with the etymological explanation of the name Stada. This word, without parallel elsewhere, is only intelligible through the explanation which the Talmud itself gives: "she proved faithless[1]." But how came the Jews in so awkward a fashion to give Mary a nickname, in which two words, which made up a sentence, were

---

[1] סטדא may perhaps be derived from סטיא דא = hebr. הסוטה אותה = this (well-known) adulteress. Cp. בן סוטדה Jer. Sanh. 25ᵈ. [G. D.]

united in one, while they had at their disposal the name Sōtā,
which was in such familiar use, that a treatise of the Mishnah
drew its name from it.' A. Fürst's[1] view is: "Mary was so-
called in reference to Numb. v. 19, since, as the Talmud itself
explains, people said, pointing the finger at her, *S'ṭath da mibba-
'alah, i.e.* she has proved unfaithful to her husband. We should
accordingly have to imagine, that, as often as Mary shewed
herself in the street, the Jews who met her aimed at her the
words *S'ṭath da.* The time at which the Jews thus began to
mock her would at the earliest be Pentecost. For Jesus in His
lifetime, as John vi. 42[2] shews, passed for the actual son of
Joseph. But when at Pentecost the preaching of the Apostles
sounded abroad concerning Jesus, the Son of God and of the
Virgin Mary, when the answer was often made to the Jews'
enquiries, that Jesus was not the son of Joseph, but conceived
of the Holy Ghost, then the logic of Jewish unbelief said: Since
God has no son, while Jesus, as the Christians themselves admit,
is not Joseph's son, it follows that he is born of Mary out of
wedlock. Mary is said[3] to have died, at the age of 59, in the fifth
year of the Emperor Claudius—certainly time enough, to allow
of her experiencing in abundance Jewish hate and insult which
will have poured itself out in stinging speeches, to the effect that
her son is a bastard and herself an adulteress. But was this
insult and hate likely to have found expression only in the single
stereotyped formula *S'ṭath da?* And it is still more difficult
to perceive how this outcry should have gradually passed over
into a proper name, so that they no more called her Miriam, but
Stada, while nevertheless, as the conversation given above
proves, the name Miriam itself was still in the memory of the
Jews at such a late period. Moreover we must not say that
Mary may have actually had both names among the Jews, and
have been called Maria Stada. For it is just this kind of name,

[1] *Saat auf Hoffnung*, 1877, S. 45.

[2] The Jews said, "Is not this Jesus, the son of Joseph, whose father and
mother we know? how doth he now say, I am come down out of heaven?"

[3] See Nicephorus Callistus, *Hist. Eccl.* ii. 3.

formed from the scoffing of the people, which is wont completely
to supplant the real name.

Accordingly it is supposable, that the nickname from its first
origin onwards was not Stada (Satda), but Ben Stada (Ben
Satda).   And in fact we always find these two words taken
together, never Stada (Satda) alone.   It is a mockery of Jesus,
which, contrary to the above-mentioned law as to the usual
effect of nicknames, has not supplanted the name Jesus, simply
for this reason that in fact the latter, as the Jewish conscience
avouches, can never be supplanted and forgotten, as well as
because the designation "son of so and so" very naturally
demands a preceding name.   But how nevertheless the nickname
strives to assert itself, is clear from this, that in the Babylonian
Talmud the expression used is always Ben Stada (Satda) only,
with the alternative, Ben Pandēra, never Jesus ben Stada, or
Jesus ben Pandēra.

A particular species of nicknames consists of caricature
names.   Under this head we are to understand such nicknames
as have arisen in dependence upon an actual name, to which by
a shifting or alteration of certain letters an odious or contemptuous meaning has been given, while the sound has remained
but little affected.   Paulus Cassel in a clever essay on caricature
names[1] has attempted to explain the expression Ben Stada as
a comic form of Ben Stara.   We will first exhibit his explanation in a somewhat improved shape, and then a conjecture of our
own.   Through the utter lack of historical foundation the origin
of this remarkable expression can never reach demonstrative
proof, but in such a case the conviction must suffice: in this or
in some similar way we can picture the thing as happening.

In *Kiddushin* 70a, it is related that once a man asked for
meat at the butchers' shops, and received the answer, "Wait, till
the servant of R. Jehudah bar J'chezkel is first served."   Thereupon the man answered, "Who is this Jehudah bar Sh'wiskel,
who has the advantage of me?"   Sh'wiskel is a comic form of

[1] *Aus Litteratur und Geschichte*, Berlin und Leipzig, 1885, pp. 323—347.

J'cheskel, and signifies, *devourer of roast meat*[1]. Such nicknames, formed by means of caricature, are found abundantly in the Talmud, rich as it is in witticisms. In *Aboda Zara* 46 a, there is even expressly given the rule for changing by caricature the names of idols and their Temples into opprobrious names; e.g. instead of *beth galja* (abode of brightness) we are to say *beth karja* (abode of pigs). In *Shabbath* 116 a[2], R. Meir calls the *evangelium* (message of salvation) *awen-gillajon* (mischievous writing), R. Jochanan *'awon-gillajon* (sinful writing); such an *awen-gillajon* or *'awon-gillajon* one is bidden not to save from the burning. The notorious false Messiah *Bar-Kokh'ba* (son of a star), was named after his overthrow *Bar kōzebā* (son of lies).

We pause beside Bar-Kokh'ba; he will build us the bridge we need to the son of Stada: Why did that pseudo-messiah call himself son of a star? Plainly in order through this very name to designate himself as the Messiah, supported by Numb. xxiv. 17, "There came forth[3] a star out of Jacob." This passage must at that time have been generally esteemed Messianic, and as such must have been held in high authority. A century earlier Herod I.[4] had caused a medal to be struck, on which a star stands above a helmet, having, according to Cassel, a like reference to Numb. xxiv. 17; many of his actions were in literal accord with this passage. (For instance he had smitten the Arabs, who dwelt in Edom; he ruled over Moab, he had success against Cleopatra ["children of Sheth[5]" was perhaps referred to Egypt, *Sethos, Sothis*].)

Also the Targums of Onkelos and Pseudo-Jonathan, the Jerusalem Talmud (Ta'anith, IV. 8), and the Midrash Rabba on Deut. i., and the Midrash on Lam. ii. 2, refer the passage in question to the king Messiah.

---

[1] שְׁוִיסָקִי = meat roasted on the spit. See *Pesach* 96 a.

[2] See (German) p. 6*, II.

[3] So Heb. דָּרַךְ (prophetic) past. Eng. Versions have future. [A. W. S.]

[4] Ordinarily called H. the Great. [A. W. S.] Illustrations are to be found e.g. in F. W. Madden, *Coins of the Jews*, London, 1881.

[5] R.V. has "sons of tumults." [A. W. S.]

To these testimonies to the lively consciousness, which the Jewish people at the turning-point of history had of the Messianic reference of the passage in Numbers, there may still however be added one, which we consider the weightiest. When the Magi came from the east, they said, "Where is the new-born king of the Jews? we have seen *his star*, and are come to worship him." If they had only said, "Where is the new-born king of the Jews?" they would have gained no credence, but would have been counted as fools. But that they should have added the reason, "We have seen *his star*," this stirred men's minds to the highest pitch. That his star had appeared was the best proof of title for the new-born king ; and this is seen from the fact that the words of the Magi received a recognition which lay at the root of the alarm. How utterly absent were all scruples from the mind of Herod, how little those scruples were removed by the doctors of the Law, the death of the children at Bethlehem gives a striking proof.

Doubtless from the commencement and onwards the history of this star continued vividly present in the memory of the Christians, inasmuch as they recognised in it the literal fulfilment of an Old Testament prophecy, and it must have been often cast up to the Jews. It is however (against Cassel) not likely that Jesus forthwith bore among Christians the name "Star," or "son of a star." The unusual designation will at the most have been used on a quite special occasion. Such an occasion we find in the appearance of the pseudo-messiah, who was named Bar Kokh'ba, i.e. son of a star. With him, whom before his overthrow the Jews took for the real Messiah foretold by Balaam, the Christians may have contrasted their Messiah, Jesus. While a R. Akiba exclaimed with passionate fervour, "Bar Kokh'ba is king Messiah," the Christians may have conceded the claim to the name "son of a star" only to Jesus of Nazareth, in whom alone the prophecy of the rising star had fulfilled itself ; and on this account Bar Kokh'ba, as Justin Martyr (*Apol.* i. 31) says, inflicted upon the Christians specially severe punishments, if they did not deny and revile *their* Messiah. It is very easily

conceivable that R. Aḳiba, who, as the Jerusalem Talmud
(Taʿanith IV. 8, p. 68 d) informs us, was especially eager to refer
the prophecy in Numbers to Bar Kokh'ba, was simply met by
the Christians with the words "Thou art in error; Jesus of
Nazareth and no other is the true son of a star," and that
R. Aḳiba on this occasion simply altered the *Ben Ṣṭara* of the
Christians into a *Ben Sṭada*, the son of a star into the son of a
harlot. For we shall again on another occasion find this R.
Aḳiba anxious to insult Jesus in the same respect. The *ṣṭara*
of the Christians would then have its rise in the Greek ἀστήρ or
the Persian *çtara* (star).

Alongside of this derivation proposed by Cassel, an attempt
at another may at least deserve mention. In the Palestinian
Talmud (*Sanhedrin*, VII. fol. 25 d at top) stands *Ben Sōṭ'da* (with
long o after s). Might not this be a parody on σωτήρ, Sōtēra,
"saviour."? The expression "mother of Sotēra" (of the Saviour)
was offensive to the Jews. The first letters *Sot* suggested Soṭa
(courtesan), and thereby the parody *Sot'da* was ready to hand.
Naturally then "mother" (Em) had to be changed into "son"
(Ben). After the origin of the parody had been forgotten, there
might easily arise through Aramaic pronunciation out of *Soṭda*
Saṭda (*Sṭada*), which the school of Pumbeditha, as stated above,
explained *S'ṭath da*.

The view of the Talmud however identifies itself with neither
the one nor the other explanation of *Ben Stada* (*Satda*). This
is clear from the passage in *Shabbath* 104 b, to which we now
revert. We are fully justified in saying that the Jews for a
long time knew absolutely nothing with certainty of *Ben Stada*.
Moreover, what is more natural than that the origin of the name,
which belongs to a chance witticism, was soon again forgotten.
The greater the delight at the wit, the less interest had the real
origin of the name. It is quite a question, whether report, as it
disseminated the new nickname, gave even once at the same time
with it the original of the same, or whether on the other hand
the Jews did not rather simply accept the designation of Jesus,
thus stamped perchance by an authority like R. Aḳiba, and were

not confused by the fact, that Jesus was also called Ben Pandēra. Both names received sanction, since the sound of the one was as hateful as that of the other was non-Jewish, and there was no desire to abandon one of those "gems." The question that would naturally suggest itself was suppressed, viz. which of the two names was genuine and which false. The more generally the two nicknames came to be adopted, the more it was for-gotten that they were nicknames, and with utter lapse of in-telligence, they were taken up quite literally, as meaning, son of an histørical Stada or Pandēra.

Yet even such names for Jesus, while gratifying the Jews by their very sound, were also destined to form the subject of further Rabbinic subtleties. In the Academy of Pumbeditha the name Stada was explained by *S'ṭath da*. Stada was thus taken as a nickname of Mary.

2.   At the end of p. 10 we said that in the passage given in *Shabbath* 104 b, there was still another remark, viz. an historical one, which needed explanation. That is the remark as to Miriam the mother of Jesus. While, that is, the New Testament knows nothing of Mary's following any particular business, the Talmud (not in this place alone) calls her a *m'gadd'la n'sajja*, i.e. "a women's hairdresser," a designation which does not tend to the honour of Jesus' mother; for re-spectable married women scarcely betook themselves to this occupation. That it is no authentic designation, but a fictitious one, may be inferred from its mention by the Talmud alone; but that work, inasmuch as it yields no glimmer of the historical circumstances connected with Jesus, cannot be con-sidered as an authoritative source. But how came the Talmud to bestow this comparatively mild insult upon the mother of Jesus, for whom elsewhere it has the characteristic designation of adulteress?

Among the women who stood near to Jesus, Mary Magdalene claims first mention. Although no stain rests upon her and her moral character, it has fallen to her lot, as Löhe in his Martyrology puts it, to be very widely accepted as the leader

and patron saint of those females, who after a life spent in the
commission of sins against the seventh commandment have had
recourse to repentance and faith.   She is wrongly held by many
to be identical with the sinner mentioned in Luke vii. 36 ff.   The
penitent Magdalene is therefore, to quote Winer's expression in
his Biblical Dictionary, an unhistorical art subject.   At what
date this mistake arose in the Christian Church, does not admit
of precise determination.   But the Talmud shews that at the
time, at which the discourse given in *Shabbath* 104 b, took place, it
had long been current among Christians.   For this very mistake,
which the Jews turned to their own account, occasioned, as we
shall see directly, a very peculiar tradition, from which again
was developed the expression Miriam *m'gadd'la.*

That Jesus' mother was named Mary, was known to the
Jews; that she had borne Jesus out of wedlock, was maintained
by them.   Then they heard a noted Christian woman of Jesus'
time often spoken of, who was named Mary of Magdala.   What
was more natural for those who had already long ceased to
ascertain more particularly at the mouth of Christians the history
of Jesus, than by this Mary (of) Magdala simply to understand
Jesus' mother, especially since their knowledge was confined to
one Mary?   She was reported to be a great sinner.   This har-
monized in a twofold way with their assumption, for, that Jesus'
mother was a sinner, was maintained by them with the utmost
certainty, and now they obtained, as they supposed, actual confirmation of this from the Christians.   Miriam (of) Magdala
was accordingly the mother of Jesus.   Whether then the Jews
found in this title an honour not appropriate for a paramour,
i.e. whether they took offence at allowing his mother to be born
in a place, from which many Rabbis were sprung[1], cannot be
determined.   In any case their mockery set itself to giving another aspect to the above-mentioned title of the mother of Jesus
by means of a parody.   Thus out of Miriam the woman of
Magdala, there came a women's hairdresser.

[1] See Lightfoot, *Centuria Chorographica*, ch. 76.

S.   2

There are still two names in our passage which need explanation ; Paphos ben Jehuda and Pandēra.

3. "Stada's (i.e. Mary's) lawful husband was Paphos
(Pappos) ben Jehudah." At first, if looked at merely from the
outside, this name presents itself through the addition "son of
Jehudah," as a genuinely historical one. Further, while the
names Stada and Pandēra are unsupported elsewhere, so that in
regard to them every unprejudiced person at once asks himself,
"Is it to be believed that any one was really so named?" the
name Paphos on the other hand is not infrequent in the Talmud
generally. P. Cassel[1] accordingly, possessed by the idea that he
is bound to seek the husband of Mary as given in the Talmud in
company with the Mary of history, maintains the view that
Paphos is the abbreviation of Josephus, and compares the Italian
Pepe or Beppo. On the other hand it is to be noted that the
abbreviation for Josephus is Jose, a very common name in the
Talmud. Comp. so early a passage as Acts iv. 36. Were it
necessary to consider our Paphos as one and the same person
with the historical Joseph, the probability of the identity would
perhaps be best established in the following way. The Paphos
of the Talmud, the Syriac Pappos, is nothing else than the Greek
πάπας, πάππας, i.e. father. In the Fathers the Pope, or the
Patriarch of Alexandria is designated by this title. Similarly
the Syriac Pappios (Greek παπίας, παππίας) "little father" is
an honourable designation of men of distinction, especially of
Bishops and other dignitaries. There was then no title of
honour which was quite so perfectly fitting for the foster father
of Jesus. If he was so named—definite testimony is wanting—
the Jews would have laid hold of this often heard Papas or Papos
as the man's real name. And thus among the Jews without
their knowledge and against their intention a member of that
Holy Family which was held by them in the deepest abhorrence,
would have received a name, which actually expressed his
dignity.

The complete ignoring of Joseph in the Apostolic letters

[1] See p. 341 of his work referred to above.

gives us but slender ground for the conclusion that they had esteemed Joseph as lightly as Protestants, provoked by the excessive honours paid him on the part of Romanists, do at the present day. So the absence of the designation Papas for Joseph in Christian literature is but slight evidence, that it was never used by Christians. But there is something else, which compels us to reject the explanation just now given. That is to say, if we allow the name Paphos ben Jehudah to bear the meaning which it has in the Talmud, the matter admits of so simple an explanation that any further enquiry must be considered as absolutely foreclosed.

Paphos (Pappus) ben Jehudah, to wit, was a contemporary of Akiba, that Rabbi, who had never seen Jesus, since he lived at a later period, but who acquired such a name for his hatred towards Him, that in the imagination of the Jews, as we shall see later, he passed as His contemporary. Accordingly Paphos also was thereby held to be a contemporary of Jesus. Now this Paphos had a wife notorious for her life of unchastity owing to the behaviour of her husband[1]. Therefore it is conceivable that this prostitute, belonging (presumably) to the time of Jesus, the only one, who lived on in the tradition, simply passed for the courtesan, of whom it was held that He was born. Accordingly the maintainer of the opinion that Stada's lawful husband was Paphos ben Jehudah, was quite right from his point of view.

4. We come now to the fourth and last name, that of *Pandēra*. In our passage the name Stada alone is a subject of difference of view. The remark that Pandēra was the paramour had been much earlier the subject of a detailed narrative. That is to say, about the year A.D. 178 the heathen Celsus, whose words Origen has preserved to us in his *Refutation* (I. 28), had received the following account from a Jew: "Mary was turned out by her husband, a carpenter by profession, after she had been convicted of unfaithfulness. Cast off by her spouse, and wandering about in disgrace, she then in obscurity gave birth to Jesus by a certain soldier Panthēra." We must connect this

[1] *Gittin* 90 a. See p. 26 below.

Jewish narrative in Celsus with the accounts of Jesus in the Talmud; for it was doubtless current among the Jews of Talmudic times, and only the scantiness of oral tradition, added to the circumstance that this tradition received no early treatment from any Rabbi[1], has occasioned its having after a hundred years shrivelled to the brief notice of the form which appears in our passage.

What marks this narrative in contrast with almost all Talmudic accounts of Jesus is this, that it contains no item, which in itself would be historically impossible. A thing might very well take place in precisely this manner in all respects. What further distinguishes it from the other narratives of the Talmud about Christ is the several more or less close correspondences with the gospel history. We call to mind the "carpenter" who is otherwise unknown to the Talmud, the "turning out" of Mary, evidently a Jewish perversion of the fact mentioned in Matt. i. 19, lastly, the "obscurity" in which Jesus was born. Such correspondences point to a time, at which the Jews had not yet lost every thread of the actual history of Jesus. But on the other hand, to how large an extent their own imagination was already responsible for the history is proved by the peculiar features, which cannot even be taken as distortions of the New Testament accounts. So long as a living

---

[1] There may however be mentioned here the narrative of Miriam, daughter of Bilga, which is found in substantially identical terms in the Jerus. Talmud, *Sukka*, 55 d, in the Bab. Talmud, *Sukka*, 56 b, in Tosephta, *Sukka*, IV. 28. That setting back of the priestly course of Bilga in the Temple compared to other priestly courses, is said to rest upon the following incident, as it is depicted in the Tosephta. It happened namely on account of Miriam, a daughter of Bilga, who fell away from the faith (שנישתמדה), and went and joined herself in marriage to a soldier of the king of Javan (Greece); and when the Greeks forced their way into the Temple, Miriam went and beat upon the surface of the altar, and called to him, Wolf, wolf (an opprobrious epithet for a non-Jew), thou hast overthrown the possession of Israel, and hast not aided her in the time of need." I should add however that the course of Bilga, according to Eleazar ben Ḳalir (cp. Zunz, *Litteraturgeschichte der synagogalen Poesie*, p. 603), is not that which had its dwelling in Nazareth. [G. D.]

connexion with the history is maintained, whatever be the difference of conception, there must prevail a consonance as to facts, whether the pen of the narrator be guided by good or by ill will. A casting out of devils e.g. was admitted by Jews no less than by Christians; but by the latter it was referred to the working of divine power, while by the others it was explained as sorcery. And if the Jews after Pentecost set up the dogma of the unchastity of Mary and the birth of Jesus out of wedlock, this is primarily a Jewish explanation of the fact, inconceivable by any human intellect, viz., the marvellous Conception and Birth of Jesus. Man's intellect had simply no choice but to reduce the history which surpassed his comprehension to the limits of natural possibility (cp. p. 11 above). But if then the Jews at the time of Celsus wish to know more than that Jesus, as not begotten by Joseph, is doubtless a bastard, if they are able to specify the more immediate circumstances of the unfaithfulness of Mary, and indeed the name of her paramour, this is no longer the Jewish conception of the history related by the Evangelists, but an invention of the uncontrolled imagination.

The most striking points here are the name and the condition of the paramour. Which of these two items established itself first in the tradition? the name or the condition? For that both things were invented by one and the same author, is unlikely for this reason that, if we assume that the word "soldier" was the first that came into the inventor's mind, the affront was so fully meted out, that, as a matter of psychology it is not conceivable that he should not have been content with it, but should have further sought a name, which represented nothing more than simply a foreign sounding appellation, such as there was no scarcity of among the Jews[1]. If on the other hand the name formed the first item in the invention, then again as a matter of psychology it is not conceivable, that the inoffensive person, who merely took an interest in giving the anonymous paramour a name, himself devised the "soldier" in addition.

[1] Zunz, *Schriften*, II. pp. 5, 6, has put together a list of Greek names borne by Jews before the reign of Herod I.

"Soldier," namely, Roman soldier, expresses, that is to say, the basest person possible, a man, who was hated and at the same time despised. In the Talmud no people have a name so hated as the Romans, who destroyed the Jews' holy city and took from them the last remnant of independence. But the accursed instrument of the Roman people for the subjugation of the Jews was the Roman army, and again the most despicable individual in this army was plainly a common soldier. If Jesus passed for a contemporary of Aḳiba, and so of the insurrection of Bar-Kokh'ba and of the persecutions on the part of Rome, which ended in this; then the discovery that He was begotten of a Roman soldier lay pretty near at hand. This discovery contained then such an amount of biting scorn, and of insult scarcely to be surpassed, that, as we said, it is as a matter of psychology impossible, that the inventor should further have desired to give the soldier a name like this, which is absolutely without odious signification (at any rate the learned men of Pumbeditha intend no such signification in the name). But just for this reason, since for the Jew of the Talmud nothing lies hidden in the name Pandēra, it is moreover inconceivable, that in later times a Jew would have held it important, to give this name to the "soldier," a word the significance of which could, we know, never be forgotten. Neither the inventor of the "soldier," nor any later period can have had a motive or interest in amending this "soldier," in completing him after a meaningless fashion.

How then? Are we thereby led at all to conclude that the word Pandēra is to be struck out of the writings of Celsus, out of Epiphanius, John of Damascus (see Cassel, p. 323), as well as the Talmudic documents? That is impossible; for, as our discussion shews, the tradition about the "soldier" was lost, earlier than the name of the paramour; so firmly rooted was the latter among the Jewish people. Since therefore we cannot form any theory, if we start with the name Pandēra, we must look at the word with the enquiry, whether it might not have been originally an appellative with a signification answering to

the Talmudic views about Jesus, which then in accordance with
the customary fashion became a proper name, whose origin and
significance disappeared from men's consciousness. What then
does Pandēra as an appellative signify? Pandēra, or, as it is
written, *Pantēra, Pantērē*, answers exactly to the Greek πάνθηρ.
What then was intended to be expressed by the designation
"Son of the panther," from which there came later, "Son of
Panther"? We answer, "Son of the Panther" meant "Son of
sensuality[1]."

But how was the panther a symbol of sensuality? In the
first place the Jews had in their sacred Books a prophecy, in
which the Grecian world-empire is represented under the figure
of a panther (cp. also Apoc. xiii. 2). In Dan. vii. 6, it is true,
the beast represents in the first place a different idea from that
of sensuality, if by this emblem there is above all stamped upon
the world-empire the character of "rapacity and of bounding
agility, with which the beast overtakes its prey" (Keil's Commentary *in loc.*). Still the wantonness and sensuality of the Greek
world, which the Jews had before their eyes, simply transcended
all limits. So much was this the case, that in fact sensuality in
the form which we notice as referred to in St Paul's Epistles,
and in particular in the first chapter of the Epistle to the
Romans, was for the Jew, who alone among the nations of that
time had still preserved a horror of this sin, the most prominent
characteristic of Greek heathenism. But among the Greeks the

---

[1] Πάνδαρος is a Greek proper name. קְלָא פְּנְדָּר is also the name of one
among the supreme judges of Sodom (*B'reshith Rabba*, 49, ed. of Constant.,
1512). It is however possible that פְּנְדְּרָא was meant to remind of πάνθηρ,
the panther. [קְלָאפְנְדָּר seems to be the Greek σκολόπενδρα. H. L. S.]
According to the belief of the ancients the panther chooses his mate among
other kinds of animals. The offspring of panther and lioness is the leopard.
See also what is said *Kiddushin* 70a on the נָמֵר. The son of the panther is
the same as the son of an illegitimate connexion, a bastard. Epiphanius[a]
says that Panther was the surname of Joseph and Klopas, the sons of Jacob.
Panther was then an old epithet of the father of Christ. [G. D.]

[a] "Οὗτος μὲν γὰρ ὁ Ἰωσὴφ ἀδελφὸς γίνεται τοῦ Κλωπᾶ, ἦν δὲ υἱὸς τοῦ Ἰακώβ, ἐπίκλην δὲ
Πάνθηρ καλουμένου. Ἀμφότεροι οὗτοι ἀπὸ τοῦ Πάνθηρος ἐπίκλην γεννῶνται." Haeres. 78,
c. 7, ed. Migne, p. 1039. [A. W. S.]

sins of the flesh were associated with the cult of Dionysos. Now
the panther among and before all other beasts was sacred to
Dionysos. He was the beast belonging to the Bacchic worship.
The worshippers slept on panther skins. It is the panther
which mainly appears upon coins exhibiting Bacchus[1]. There
was a special form of this coin, in which Bacchus stands before a panther and gives him wine to drink (Cassel, p. 336).
Taking this into consideration, we have no difficulty in understanding it, if the Jews, when they read Dan. vii., thought
of the beast sacred to Dionysos and of the sensuality which belonged to his cult. Thus by the expression "Son of the Panther"
they meant to convey that Jesus was born of unchastity in the
form in which it appears only among the Greeks ; i.e. that He
was sprung from the grossest unchastity.

But now there arises the question ; How came Jesus to be
given a nickname drawn from a circle of ideas lying so far from
the beaten track ? We answer : plainly a special motive must
have presented itself for designating Jesus precisely thus and not
otherwise. Nitzsch[2] has recognised in Pandēra a mutilated
form of $\pi\alpha\rho\theta\acute{\epsilon}\nu\sigma$, virgin, except that he took Pandēra not as the
Greek $\pi\acute{\alpha}\nu\theta\eta\rho$ but as $\pi\alpha\nu\theta\acute{\eta}\rho\alpha$, of which he maintains—I know
not how truly—that it answers to the Latin *lupa*, courtesan.
Cp. also Cassel, pp. 334 f.   From "Son of the Virgin," a hostile
wit has made, "Son of the beast of wantonness."

Moreover Mary was not herself on any occasion called as a
nickname "pandēra" (beast of wantonness), however fitly, according to Jewish conceptions, she might have been so designated. For this parody is never found but in connexion with
Ben (*Bar*) "son."   The hatred and scorn of the Jews was always
aimed principally at the person of Jesus Himself. Thus *pantera*
did not arise out of *parthena* (with an Aramaic ending), but
out of *Ben Parthena* was formed *Ben Pandera*, a jeer which

---

[1] See F. W. Madden, *Dict. of Roman Coins*, London, 1889, p. 119 f.
For illustrative gems see C. W. King's *Antique Gems and Rings*, London,
1872, ii. plate xxvii with description, p. 56. [A. W. S.]

[2] Appendix to Bleek in *Theol. Studien u. Kritiken*, 1840, p. 116.

was too pointed not to be welcomed and disseminated. Only the expression, just as Ben Stada (Satda), and as nicknames in general, was destined to become a formal proper name, whose character after some time came to be so little understood, that they proceeded to give this Pandēra thus changed to a masculine sense a status worthy of his son.

The origin of the "soldier" we must remove to the time between the war with Hadrian and Celsus. For, as has been already noticed above, the "soldier" owes his existence to the terrible bitterness towards the Romans aroused by that war; on the other hand the whole story evidently appertains to a time in which the Jews had already ceased to have intercourse with the Christians, and in which, giving free rein to caprice and to a spiteful imagination, they merely built upon the remains of tradition. All this tallies with a generation which is subsequent to R. Akiba, and is moulded by him.

The form of parody "Ben Pandēra" on the other hand is to be placed at the time, when the Jews did not yet capriciously invent, but only disfigured and, when possible, caricatured the facts of the Gospel as emphasized by the Christians, with whom they were still in contact. This was the very time of Akiba, in which according to our earlier deduction the designation Ben Stada (Satda) also may have arisen.

CHARACTER OF THE MOTHER OF JESUS.

Just as in the Christian Church the mother of the Saviour has been gradually advanced to such honours that in one part of it she is taken to have been sinless as the Lord Jesus Christ Himself; so by the bitterest foes of the Church, the Jews, she, the blessed among women, has been overlaid with the deepest contumely. As mother of Jesus she shared the hatred and mockery, which He had to experience. We have seen above (p. 9) that Jesus was taken for a bastard, who was conceived out of wedlock by the espoused Mary. Now we come to consider a passage, which gives Mary the general character of unchastity.

Gittin 90 a[1], "There is a tradition, R. Meir used to say : Just as there are various kinds of taste as regards eating, so there are also various dispositions as regards women. There is the man into whose cup a fly falls[2] and he casts it out, but all the same he does not drink it (the cup). Such was the manner of Paphos ben Jehudah, who used to lock the door upon his wife, and go out."

The sense of the comparison is clear.

Thus Paphos ben Jehudah dealt with his wife[3]. But is there any word of censure spoken here against the wife of Paphos? In point of fact the passage in the Talmud which we are considering, has to do solely with Paphos, against whom it is brought as a reproach, that he kept himself separate from his wife. Also we are safe in assuming that R. Meir's saying would not have been transmitted, if it had not been distinguished through the singular symbolism in which it is clothed. It was not till later that Paphos became a person frequently named, when people had come to see in him the husband of Jesus' mother. Thereupon there must have entered into the Jewish conception of our passage a new element, and one originally altogether foreign to it. The passage was considered in its relation to Jesus, whose mother was that woman thus treated by her husband. And accordingly out of the notice as to Paphos there was formed a story about Mary. In connexion with the idea, that Mary conceived Jesus out of wedlock, our Talmud-passage was taken up as an incomplete piece of a character-sketch of Mary, which pointed out the cause how

---

[1] See (German) p. 6*, III.

[2] The expression זבוב בקערה, a fly in the dish, is explained by Gitt. 6 b. [G. D.]

[3] A fly falls into the cup—some suspicion had befallen the wife of Paphos. Since that time he had no more intercourse with her, and shut her off also from any other intercourse. Rashi maintains that this treatment has made her an actual adulteress, which she was not hitherto. [G. D.]

Mary came to be a prostitute. It would not be difficult for us accordingly to complete the *Gittin* passage in that sense. But we are relieved from this by the explanation of Rashi (ob. A.D. 1105), the purport of which is naturally no discovery of Rashi's, but belongs to the old time, in which Paphos passed as Mary's husband. Rashi comments thus upon our passage: "Paphos ben Jehudah was the husband of Mary, the women's hairdresser. Whenever he went out of his house into the street, he locked the door upon her, that no one might be able to speak with her. And that is a course which became him not; for on this account there arose enmity between them, and she in wantonness broke her faith with her husband."

Our passage, whose original sense cannot be binding for us, inasmuch as soon enough—for the discourse of *Shabbath* 104 b puts before us the conception which Rashi shares—it was supplanted by the other, which has thenceforward been believed by the Jews, is the only one which gives to the special reproach that Mary had conceived Jesus out of wedlock, the wider turn, that in consequence of her husband's conduct she had led a generally unchaste life. Not only once had she transgressed, but continually, since she broke through the barriers set by her husband. Jesus was born—so our passage tacitly asserts—of one habitually unfaithful.

A LEGEND CONCERNING MARY.

Any account, which is peculiar to the Talmud, concerning Jesus and His mother, belongs, it is true, to the reign of myth, so that even such a foe of Jesus as David Frederick Strauss, on the whole disdained to meddle with those accounts. But while the preceding narratives are not as far as their import is concerned intrinsically impossible, the following one bears from beginning to end upon its face the stamp of fable.

Chagigah 4 b[1]: "The Angel of death was found with R.

---

[1] See (German) p. 6*, IV. (a).

Bibi bar Abbai[1]. The former said to his attendant, Go, bring
me Miriam the women's hairdresser. He went and brought him
Miriam the children's teacher. The Angel of death said to him,
I said, Miriam the women's hairdresser. The messenger said to
him, Then I will bring her [the other] back. The Angel of death
said to him, Since thou hast brought her, let her be reckoned
(among the dead)."

This story R. Joseph[2] adduces in support of Prov. xiii. 23
"Many a one is snatched away without judgment." "Is it a fact
then," said R. Joseph to his pupils, "that any one must go hence
before his time? Certainly, for so and so has befallen the
children's teacher, Miriam." While Miriam the women's hairdresser ought to have died, she remained alive, and instead of
her the other Miriam, who was not appointed to die, was brought
by the messenger of the Angel of death. How then it came
about, that the Angel of death sent his messenger to bring
Miriam the women's hairdresser, the Talmud intimates briefly
in the words "The Angel of death was with R. Bibi bar Abbai."
A conversation had thus arisen between them, after which the
Angel gave the order mentioned. It is easy to conjecture in
what spirit R. Bibi had spoken. The assumption that he had
requested the Angel to put an end to Mary's life is confirmed on
a closer investigation of the origin of this legend.

The unsatisfactory ending of the story at once invites such an
investigation. For this asserts, we see, nothing else than that
Mary the women's hairdresser in consequence of the error of the
messenger had experienced the good fortune to continue in life
longer than had been appointed for her. But how—we must
ask—does the Talmud come to speak of a piece of good fortune
as happening to this woman?

Inasmuch as R. Bibi lived in the 4th century of the Christian
era, he can neither have seen Mary nor been her contemporary.

---

[1] He flourished in the 4th century.

[2] More fully, Joseph bar Chia, born at Shili in Babylonia, A.D. 259. He
was head of the Academy at Pumbeditha, and in his later years, though blind,
composed a Targum on the Hagiographa. [A. W. S.]

Nevertheless he was able to say that he desired Mary's death and the extinction of her name and memory. When in his time, as it appears, a much beloved Jewess, Miriam the children's teacher by name, died and her death was mourned as premature, both generally and in particular by R. Bibi, then he may have exclaimed ; Why had she to die so early while the accursed Miriam lives on ? This lament for the dead on R. Bibi's part was disseminated, but in such a way, that in the representation of it the Mary to whom he wished (eternal) death, was thought of as living in his time, and his observation, that the excellent Mary must needs die, while the infamous Mary still lived on, was understood as though the messenger of death had made a mistake ; so that finally R. Bibi's wish for death for the latter was construed as though it had taken place in personal intercourse with the Angel of death.

We have already remarked at an early stage, and shall have occasion to do so again, that the Talmud, in relation to Jesus, has no conception of chronology, and indeed, the later the origin of notices about Jesus, the more reckless are they in their chronological lapses. The post-talmudic Targum Sheni on the Book of Esther actually reckons Jesus among the ancestors of Haman, an anachronism, which Levy in his Dictionary of the Targums (I. p. 330) in vain seeks to justify. In the face of such an unfathomable error what signifies the erroneous representation that R. Bibi lived in the time of Mary ? The Talmudic commentary Tosaphoth on *Chagigah* 4 b remarks[1] : "The Angel of death was with R. Bibi, and related to him the history of Miriam the women's hairdresser, which took place in the time of the second Temple. This Miriam was the mother of that *so and so* [i.e. Jesus], as is to be read in *Shabbath* 104 b." But the wording of the Talmud says quite distinctly that Mary lived in the very time of R. Bibi, on which account the Angel of death spoke with him not of one who had existed earlier, but of one actually living. Further this Angel, we may note, at that very time in the

[1] See (German) p. 6*, IV. (b).

presence of R. Bibi commissions his messenger, to bring her, i.e. to deliver her to death. The Tosaphoth notes on *Shabbath* 104 b[1] seek needlessly to remove the anachronism by the assumption that there were two women's hairdressers, named Mary. At any rate we may adduce one further passage from the Jerusalem Talmud, which shews us a Mary, daughter of Eli, in hell. The Talmud itself makes it clear that this Mary is not the mother of Jesus : otherwise it would have substituted a different transgression on her part from that of an irreligious practice of fasting. In the Jerusalem *Chagigah* 77 d[2], a devout person relates that he saw in a dream various punishments in hell. " He saw also Miriam, the daughter of Eli Betzalim, suspended, as R. Lazar ben Jose says, by the paps of her breasts. R. Jose ben Chanina[3] says : The hinge of hell's gate was fastened in her ear. He said to them [? the angels of punishment], Why is this done to her ? The answer was, Because she fasted and published the fact. Others said, Because she fasted one day, and counted two days (of feasting) as a set off. He asked them, How long shall she be so ? They answered him, Until Shim'on ben Shetach comes ; then we shall take it out of her ear and put it into his ear."

TWO DECLARATIONS WITH REGARD TO THE ILLEGITIMATE BIRTH OF JESUS.

A. *The pretended record.*

It is well known to us not only from the Old Testament but also from the New, what significance attached to the family pedigree among the Jews. Of special importance were the priestly pedigrees and the genealogies of the royal house. The former were for the most part brought back with them from the Babylonish exile, and carefully preserved and continued ; of the

---

[1] See p. 7*, IV. (c).

[2] See p. 18*, XXII.

[3] A contemporary of Akiba.

latter the Book of Ruth, the Chronicles, and the Gospels give samples. King Herod I. is said to have destroyed all official pedigrees extant in his time, a statement of Eusebius[1] which Winer[2] perhaps wrongly doubts. Hamburger[3] not without probability attributes to this measure of Herod the aim of thereby blotting out the recollection of his own humble origin and breaking down the ancestral pride of the Jews. And this is evidently the intention of the Talmud, when[4] it puts into the mouth of the Amoræan R. Rami, son of R. Joden, in the name of Rab, the following declaration: "Since the book of genealogies was hidden, the power of the learned has been crippled and the light of their eyes (knowledge) darkened." But on the other hand it is certain that individual men of learning transmitted to their scholars what they had preserved in their memories from those perished lists, so that there were family genealogies which did not meet the fate of the public ones. Accordingly there is thus mentioned from the time after the destruction of Jerusalem a 'book of genealogies' (*J'bamoth* 49 b), which, it is highly probable, contained a collection of all the extant remains of genealogies which were surviving in either a written or oral form. That this collection (cp. as early a passage as Gen. iv. 17, 20 ff.) was interwoven with more or less closely connected notices, is proved by the fragments preserved, of which at present only the following one concerns us.

It is said, namely in the Mishnah, *J'bamoth* 49 a[5] (Mishnah IV. 13 ; cp. 49 b) "Simeon ben Azzai[6] has said: I found in Jerusalem a book of genealogies; therein was written : That so and so is a bastard son of a married woman."

---

[1] *Eccles. Hist.* i. 7 (quoting Africanus). See Bright's Eus. *E. H.* Oxford, 1872, p. 21. [A. W. S.]

[2] *Bibl. Realwörterbuch,* II. p. 516.

[3] *Real-Encyclopädie für Bibel u. Thalmud,* II. p. 294.

[4] *P'sachim,* 62 b.

[5] See p. 7*, VI.

[6] A contemporary of Akiba, and skilled in the Law, though not, strictly speaking, a Rabbi, as not having been ordained. [A. W. S.]

Frederick Louis Jahn was in the habit of never speaking of the first Napoleon, as long as he was in power, by his name, but of designating him by a significant "he." The reason for such a periphrasis was aversion to that person, joined with a certain dread of painting the devil upon the wall. Still stronger is the hatred of the Jewish people towards Jesus. Eisenmenger in the second chapter of the first part of his *Entdecktes Judenthum* has adduced twenty-eight periphrastic titles of Jesus from Jewish writings. One of these designations is *otho ha'ish* "that man," "so and so." Most of these however have their origin in post-talmudic times, in which, as a consequence of the oppression on the part of the Christians, the hatred towards Jesus, which since the Crucifixion and rejection of the Son of God has lain deep in the soul of the Jews, was kindled to the fullest extent. The Talmudic period knows nothing of severity on the part of the Christians; accordingly this motive failed to evoke any excessive measure of hostility towards Jesus. Still in the time of Akiba or Bar Kokh'ba there was a strong feeling against Jesus. We may therefore expect from it specially strong expressions of Jewish hostility. The origin of the nickname Ben Stada is to be referred to this time (see above, p. 15). Simeon ben Azzai was a pupil and colleague of Akiba. Several Talmudic passages bear witness to his combative attitude towards the Minim (Judæo-Christians)[1], cp. *Hamburger*, ii. p. 1120.

By the "so and so" here mentioned can only be meant Jesus, for there was no one else for whom the Jews had so characteristically kept the predicate *mamzēr*, bastard, no one to whom they had more willingly ascribed it.

Accordingly to every Jew, and in particular to the pupils of Akiba, this doctrine of the bastardy of Jesus was simply a fundamental truth even as the " Conceived of the Holy Ghost, Born of the Virgin Mary " is to every Christian, even if he has never

---

[1] This word does not however appear to be always confined to Christian proselytes from Judaism. See '*Aboda Zara* in Ewald's (German) translation, p. 190, with his note on p. 121, collecting passages from Rashi and others. See also Kohut's *Aruch*, s.v. [A. W. S.]

had a Bible in his hand (and we know that there are a fair
number of such). But just as Luther was beyond measure
delighted when he received into his hands the sacred records,
which confirmed for him that which he already knew, and related
much more beside, so a foe of Jesus like Ben Azzai must have
been highly charmed when he found in Jerusalem, then lying in
ruins, a Jewish document, no matter of what degree of credibility,
in which was written "Jesus the Nazarene [Ben Azzai substituted *so and so*] a bastard son of a married woman." This *find*
was valuable enough for Ben Azzai to communicate it to his
pupils, who for their part were not slack in giving the discovery
a wider circulation[1].

B.   *The pretended evidence of Mary herself.*

There can be only one authentic human testimony as to the
birth of Jesus, viz. the testimony of the mother of Jesus herself.
From the mouth of Mary springs directly or indirectly the information which we read in the commencement of the Gospel
of St Luke. From the mouth of none other than this parent,
according to the Talmud, R. Akiba pretends to have drawn the
secret of the illegitimate birth of Jesus. *Kallah* 18 b[2]. "A
shameless person is according to R. Eliezer[3] a bastard, according
to R. Joshua[4] a son of a woman in her separation, according to
R. Akiba, a bastard *and* son of a woman in her separation.
Once there sat elders at the gate when two boys passed by;

---

[1] In the Mishnah Jebamoth, iv. 13, the subject is the definition of the
notion of "bastard," towards which that treatise contributed a striking
illustration. Whether Jesus was therein referred to may be questioned.
[G. D.]

[2] See (German) p. 7*, vii.

[3] The name when thus used absolutely stands for Eliezer ben Hyrkanus,
teacher of Akiba, and founder of the Academy at Lud. [A. W. S.]

[4] His full name was Joshua ben Chanania. He was a disciple of Jochanan
ben Zakkai, who died about A.D. 70, and vice-president in the presidency of
Gamaliel (A.D. 80—115). See story of him in *Chagigah* 5 b. [A. W. S.]

S.   3

one had his head covered, the other bare[1]. Of him who had
his head uncovered, R. Eliezer said, 'A bastard!' R. Joshua
said, 'A son of a woman in her separation,' R. Akiba said, 'A
bastard *and* son of a woman in her separation.' They said to
R. Akiba, 'How has thine heart impelled thee to the audacity
of contradicting the words of thy colleagues?' He said to them,
'I am about to prove it.' Thereupon he went to the boy's
mother, and found her sitting in the market and selling pulse.
He said to her, 'My daughter, if thou tellest me the thing
which I ask thee, I will bring thee to eternal life.' She said
to him, 'Swear it to me!' Thereupon R. Akiba took the oath
with his lips, while he cancelled it in his heart. Then said he
to her, 'Of what sort is this thy son?' She said to him, 'When
I betook myself to the bridal chamber, I was in my separation,
and my husband stayed away from me. But my paranymph
came to me, and by him I have this son.' So the boy was dis-
covered to be both a bastard and the son of a woman in her
separation. Thereupon said they, 'Great is R. Akiba, in that
he has put to shame his teachers.' In the same hour they said,
'Blessed be the Lord God of Israel, Who hath revealed His
secret to R. Akiba ben Joseph.'"

Neither the name of the son nor that of the mother is here
mentioned. But both from the *Sepher Tōl'dōth Jeshu* (Book of
the History of Jesus) published by J. Chr. Wagenseil (*Tela ignea
Satanae*, Altdorf, 1681, vol. II.) and from that of J. J. Huldreich
(Leyden, 1705) it plainly follows that the Jews had in mind
Jesus and His mother. And moreover Lichtenstein in his
Hebrew treatise *Sepher Tōl'dōth Jeshua'* remarks, "I have heard
in my youth from Rabbis of consideration, that in the treatise
Kallah there is an allusion to that man (Jesus)." Chr. Schöttgen[2]
thinks that the names were erased either by the Jews through

---

[1] "To go bareheaded was considered not only unwholesome, but so in-
decorous, that an uncovered head is a figurative expression for coarseness,
shamelessness, and impudence." Franz Delitzsch, *Ein Tag in Capernaum*
(*A Day in Capernaum*), p. 150. [H. L. S.]

[2] *Horae Hebraicae et Talmudicae*, II. p. 696.

fear, or by the Pope's censors. But the censors must have
found the passage in the form in which it now reads; for
the men who were so liberal in erasures that they cancelled
the whole treatise *Aboda Zara*[1], would certainly have erased
in *Kallah* not only the names, but the whole account, if they
had there come upon the names Jesus and Mary[2]. And that
the names were removed by the Jews through fear appears to us
improbable for this reason that we can find no motive for their
mutilating this passage only, while they allowed other mentions
of Jesus and Mary to stand.

We believe accordingly that the account stood in the Talmud
from the very beginning without the name of the mother or of
the boy, and so our question runs thus: Are the Jews right, and
do they hit the meaning of the Talmud, when they refer the
passage to Jesus? We answer: They are right, but nevertheless
they do not hit the meaning of the Talmud. For the Talmud,
as introducing no name and not even once hinting at it, clearly
knows none. The thought of Jesus was kept out of the author's
view by the mention of the mother's position. Mary passes, as
we know, in the Talmud for a women's hairdresser, but here
she appears as a dealer in pulse. The very position here assigned to the mother will have been the cause of the names
being soon lost or struck out as erroneous by the author; on the
other hand it appears to point to an early origin of our narrative.
Of the "soldier" Pandēra (see above, p. 19 ff.) the individual
narrator still, as it appears, knew nothing; accordingly the little
story is probably to be dated prior to the year A.D. 178.

The proof then, that our narrative treats of Jesus, must arise
from its contents. Only we must not allow ourselves to be
biassed by the introductory sentence, through which the narrative not only has become inconsistent, but also has received a

---

[1] See Strack, *Einleitung in den Thalmud*, p. 52.

[2] Also in the text of the treatise *Kallah* published by N. Coronel in accordance with a much fuller recension no names are mentioned. See *Commentarios quinque doctrinam talmudicam illustrantes...edidit N. C.*, Vienna,
1864, p. 3 b.

wholly different turn, from what it originally possessed—the sentence, namely, that the three Rabbis had asserted of any shameless person that he was of ignominious origin, but were not at one as regards the degree of ignominy. Lichtenstein rightly says : " How many bastards then are there at the present moment in Israel, who go with uncovered head ! " The Talmudic writer has taken up the traditional account, as though the three Rabbis had given judgment in the manner specified as to *every* shameless person.

And the narrative appears to have a wholly different point. If we consider it without the introduction we have mentioned, the following took place. When a boy with head uncovered passed by the Rabbis, R. Eliezer exclaimed, " A bastard ! " By this he did not mean to say, " From his shamelessness I recognise him to be a bastard," but "His bad extraction brings these bad manners with it." Plainly he knew the boy and considered him already before this occurrence to be a bastard. The other Rabbi, who likewise knew the boy, gave still sharper expression to his displeasure at his shamelessness ; for " son of a woman in her separation" is to be judged in accordance with Lev. xx. 18, where the punishment of death is appointed for intercourse with such. Also R. Joshua did not mean that the boy through his shamelessness had betrayed himself as the son of such a woman, but that any one who was of such ignominious birth, could not fail to behave himself thus shamelessly. R. Akiba objects to his colleagues : "Ye still judge this lad too favourably : he is a bastard and son of a woman in her separation as well." It appears then singular that both the colleagues of R. Akiba took his objection ill ; the more strange since afterwards they praise him, because his opinion is the true one. The aim of the Talmudic writer in this version of the story was simple, viz. that R. Akiba through the reproving observation of his colleagues, might obtain an opportunity to enter upon the weighty proof by means of facts, that he alone was right, i.e. that the boy was of the most disgraceful origin possible. When the proof had turned out so absolutely clear a one, his colleagues rejoice and praise God for having disclosed His secret to R. Akiba.

If the boy's shamelessness only formed the outward occasion for
the Rabbis' conversation with regard to his disgraceful birth,
this last, as already indicated, must have been long an object of
offence to them. Nay, that they discussed the matter so very
eagerly shews that the boy must have had an unusual importance
for them; he must have been peculiarly hated by them, more
hated than other boys who behaved themselves shamelessly and
passed for illegitimate children, such as no doubt there have
always been here and there in Israel. Moreover the joy of both
the other Rabbis over the victory of R. Akiba is striking. We
have a right to ask after the special causes of such special hatred.
What are these causes? I answer: Tell me the name of the boy,
and the causes are plain as daylight. But since the Talmud
mentions no name, we must enquire further, Who can the boy
have been? No one's baseness of origin is so eagerly emphasized
and discussed in the Talmud as that of Jesus. On no one does
the Talmud seek with such zeal and so much skill in many ways
to stamp the character of bastard as on Jesus, who is to it the
bastard *par excellence*. Proof of this may be found in the passages
of the Talmud referring to Jesus which have been already discussed. Accordingly those persons, whether Jews or Christians,
are perfectly right, who explained the above quoted passage of
the Talmud as relating to Jesus.

But—some one might ask—how is it possible to understand
Jesus by the boy, when R. Akiba, to whose time the story is
represented as belonging, lived about a century after Him, and
thus can never have seen Jesus, and least of all as a boy? We
have here again (cp. pp. 19, 22, 29) to deal with an anachronism,
not with an accidental and wholly unfounded one, but with one
that is very peculiar, which straightway furnishes us with a
further proof that the boy must be none other than Jesus. We
lay our finger on the name Akiba, and at the same time call to
mind the following facts.

In a passage of the Talmud (*Sanhedrin* 67 a[1]) to be quoted in
the third division of our treatise, it is said that Jesus was crucified

[1] See p. 5*, I. (b).

at Lud (Lydda), an assertion, which naturally is read with the
utmost astonishment, if not by the Jews who swear by the
Talmud, at least by Christians, and which, as it seems, has been
up to this time unintelligible.   It appears scarcely credible that
the very place of Jesus' Crucifixion, this most memorable event
in His whole story, has been forgotten by the Jews.   And yet so
it is : Jesus according to the Talmud was crucified not in Jerusalem but in Lud.   How is this to be explained?   Naturally we
must not think of a confusion through error, of a lapse of memory.
No : the removal of the Crucifixion of Jesus to Lud, this place
which nowhere occurs in the New Testament accounts of the story
of Jesus[1], betrays utter lack of acquaintance with the history.   And
yet this assertion of the Talmud must have a foundation.   We
believe that we can find this foundation only in the following
assumption ; Lud became for the Jews a centre for accounts of
Jesus, i.e. nowhere was there more related about Jesus than at
Lud, so that later generations received the impression that these
occurrences, the accounts of which were derived thence, took place
in Lud itself.   The circumstance that R. Akiba was a teacher
at Lud supports the view that Lud is really to be looked upon as
the source of several accounts of Jesus ; for as to R. Akiba we
know what great celebrity he possessed as a Rabbi, as well as
also what passionate hatred of Jesus dwelt within this admirer of
Bar Kokh'ba.   That the effect of R. Akiba's controversial attitude
towards Christianity was no light one for his adherents may be
conjectured *a priori*.   But a stronger effect cannot be conceived
than that Akiba on account of his vehement attacks upon Jesus
was taken in later times for a contemporary, who had lived with
Him in one and the same town.   For to say that Jesus was
crucified in Lud means nothing else than that He was crucified in
Akiba's city in the time of the man who according to the Jews'
view was one of those most accurately acquainted with the history
of Jesus.   In Lud also the narrative contained in *Kallah* 18 b,
must have its origin.

---

[1] Although mentioned in Acts ix. 32, 35, 38.   [A. W. S.]

To conclude, it only now remains to take a survey of the rise of this Jesus-legend. It owes its origin doubtless to the natural eagerness of the Jews to know and therefore also to tell details upon the subject, to them most important and interesting, of the illegitimate birth of Jesus. The pith of the story in its oldest form may have been built up of the following elements: (1) The doctrine, perhaps already in existence before Akiba, that Jesus was son of a courtesan. (2) The proposition, that He had been shameless in His youth. Akiba in his disputes with the Christians had certainly learned much of the story of Jesus, as well as that which is related (Luke ii. 46, 47) as to the boy Jesus when twelve years old in the temple, "And all who heard him, were astonished at his understanding and his answers." When compared with the part taken by Jesus later against the lawyers, which appeared to him as pure shamelessness[1], R. Akiba found already in this story of His childhood the first traces of that shameless behaviour. (3) This also may without hesitation be assumed to be an old ingredient of the Talmudic narrative, that Akiba, who summed up and concentrated his attacks upon the person of Jesus in the reproach of a shameful origin, actually in presence of the lawyers connected with this origin the boy's shamelessness. These three constituent elements of the narrative, thus preached by Akiba, were propagated by word of mouth, and it is not to be wondered at that, after Akiba had once been taken for a contemporary of Jesus, he and his colleagues were understood to have been among the Rabbis, towards whom the boy Jesus was said to have behaved shamelessly. How that story, which we now read in the treatise *Kallah*, was gradually constructed upon these foundations by means of additions and further developments, eludes investigation. It is not impossible that matter was to some extent furnished to the Jews from the Christian side in apocryphal narratives, which the former found serviceable in support of alterations in the story in accordance with their view.

---

[1] Cp. *Gittin* 57 a (see p. 17*, xxi. (a). [G. D.]

II. THE WORKS OF JESUS.

A. *Jesus and His Teacher.* "How knoweth this man letters, having never learned?" exclaimed the Jews (John vii. 15), full of amazement at His teaching. And in Matt. xiii. 54 it says: "He taught in their synagogues[1], insomuch that they were astonished, and said, Whence hath this man this wisdom?" So Mark vi. 2: "[They] were astonished, saying, Whence hath this man these things? and, What is the wisdom that is given to this man?...Is not this the carpenter, the son of Mary?...and they were offended in him."

In contrast with these New Testament notices, according to which Jesus, without having enjoyed the tuition of a distinguished Rabbi, was full of the highest wisdom and knowledge of the Scriptures, the Talmud[2] makes Jesus to stand in the relation of disciple to R. Joshua ben P'rachyah. Nay, what is more, this statement of the Talmud is also inconsistent with the Talmud itself. For according to this (cp. *Aboth of R. Nathan,* 5 a) no child of a courtesan was allowed to come to Jerusalem and visit the schools and study, an ordinance which fully agrees with Deut. xxiii. 2: "A bastard shall not enter into the assembly of the Lord; even to the tenth generation shall none of his enter into the assembly of the Lord[3]." But we have already seen sufficiently in the first part of our work how unquestionable the Talmud considers it, that Jesus was begotten out of wedlock. Thereupon there arises the question: Did the Rabbis, who relate the history of Jesus' discipleship, know nothing of the inconsistent belief on the part of the Jews as to His origin? Before we proceed to answer this question, we must furnish the statement of the Talmud itself.

---

[1] So Luther's translation. See Brit. and For. Bible Soc.'s ed., Köln, 1851; but the original has ἐν τῇ συναγωγῇ αὐτῶν. [A. W. S.]

[2] *Sanhedrin* 107 b; *Sota* 47 a.

[3] This passage was always referred only to cases of unfaithfulness in marriage. [G. D.]

Sanhedrin 107 b[1]: The Rabbis have taught: The left should always be repelled, and the right on the other hand drawn nearer. But one should not do it... as R. Joshua ben P'rachyah, who thrust forth Jesus with both hands. What was the matter with regard to R. Joshua ben P'rachyah? When king Jannai[2] directed the destruction of the Rabbis, R. Joshua ben P'rachyah and Jesus went to Alexandria. When security returned, Rabbi Simeon ben Shetach[3] sent him a letter to this effect: "From me, Jerusalem the holy city, to thee, Alexandria in Egypt, my sister. My spouse tarries in thee, and I dwell desolate." Thereupon Joshua arose and came; and a certain inn was in his way, in which they treated him with great respect. Then spake Joshua: "How fair is this inn (Akhsanga)!" Jesus saith to him: "But, Rabbi, she (Akhsanga = a hostess) has little narrow eyes." Joshua replied: "Thou godless fellow, dost thou occupy thyself with such things?" directed that 400 horns should be brought, and put Him under strict excommunication. Jesus oftentimes came and said to him, "Take me back." Joshua did not trouble himself about Him. One day, just as Joshua was reading the sh'ma' (the words: "Hear, O Israel," Deut. vi. 4 etc.), Jesus came to him, hoping that he would take Him back. Joshua made a sign to Him with his hand. Then Jesus thought that he had altogether repulsed Him, and went away, set up a brickbat, and worshipped it. Joshua said to Him: "Be converted!" Jesus saith: "Thus have I been taught by thee: from him that sinneth and that maketh the people to sin, is taken away the possibility of repentance." And the Teacher [i.e. he, who is everywhere mentioned by this title in the Talmud] has said: "Jesus had practised sorcery and had corrupted and misled Israel." Here *Sanh.* 43 a[4] is referred to (where the words of "the Teacher" are found).

[1] For the most part in the same words as *Sota* 47a. See p. 8*, VIII., IX.

[2] For him see p. 42.

[3] For his approximate date see p. 48. He received some Greek culture through a sojourn in Alexandria. [A. W. S.]

[4] See p. 15*, xv.

The Jerusalem Talmud, which[1] relates the same story, has in place of Joshua ben P'rachyah the name of his contemporary Jehudah ben Tabbai. This makes no essential difference. The identification of the two by Hamburger (II. 1053, footnote) is ingenious. Of much more weight is another difference in the narrative of the two Talmuds; that is to say, the Babylonian Talmud gives the name of the disciple, the Jerusalem on the contrary does not mention his name,—plainly, because it does not know him. The question now is; did the Babylonian Gemara possess a less defective tradition than the Jerusalem, or has it, without possessing a more complete form of this, first introduced the name Jesus on the ground of probability?

The answer to this question we obtain from the correct explanation of the striking anachronism which the account in the text of the Babylonian Talmud contains. According to this, Jesus would have lived some hundred years *before* the actual Jesus, for king Jannai lived B.C. 104—78, and about the year B.C. 87 there took place the crucifixion of the 800 Pharisees after the capture of the stronghold Bethome[2], which was the occasion of the flight into Syria and Egypt on the part of the Pharisees generally in the country, and among them of Joshua ben P'rachyah and Jehudah ben Tabbai. Inasmuch then as the narrative bears upon its face the stamp of a genuine account, which has been disseminated indeed in a disfigured, and for that very reason in many respects obscure, shape, it is unquestionable, that the name Jesus is here spurious, and, even if it were found in all the sources of our information, would have to be struck out. But, as the case stands, the Jerusalem Talmud, as already mentioned, has not got this name, and this very circumstance, especially in view of the character[3] of this Talmud, supports our decision,

---

[1] *Chagigah*, II. 2, and *Sanhedrin*, VI. 8.

[2] See Schürer's *Hist. of the Jewish People*, Eng. Transl., Div. I. vol. I. 303; and for history of Jannai (=Alexander Jannaeus, son of John Hyrcanus I.), *ibid.* 295—307. [A. W. S.]

[3] "In Palestine there was developed a greater inclination to maintain and disseminate the old tradition than to develop it further. . . . In the Jerusalem

that the name Jesus was originally wanting, and the anachronism first arose through this later interpolation. I grant that this interpolation is old, found even before the Gemara, or, if we wish to express ourselves very cautiously, the Gemara already has referred to what is here related about Jesus. This follows from the fact that the Gemara attaches to the narrative the following addition : "The same authority, which reports this story, says elsewhere [namely in the passage, *Sanhed.* 43 a [1], to be adduced in the third part of our work]: 'Jesus had practised sorcery, and had corrupted and misled Israel.'" In this charge, which taxes Jesus with weighty offences the Gemara perceives a confirmatory parallel to that which is here related of the disciple of Joshua ben P'rachyah. The assertion that Jesus was the sinful disciple is, as already remarked, undoubtedly false ; yet we find, on close consideration of the story, several features which might lead to the assumption of identity. As such we reckon, 1st, the flight from a blood-thirsty king into Egypt. It was an account spread by the Christians themselves that Jesus once fled to Egypt from a king who had a design on His life. Cp. Matt. ii. 13—15. This account was fitted to make a sharp impression on the Jewish memory, since it plainly contains the key to the assertion that Jesus was in a position to work Egyptian sorceries. 2ndly, His behaviour towards the Rabbi. The lack of respect towards Joshua was certainly a contrast to the demeanour of Jesus in the Gospels towards the Rabbinic authorities [2]; but we know from *Kallah* 18 b, that Jesus passed for a shameless person, and in *Gittin* 57 a [3] (see later) we read that on account of His shamelessness towards the doctors of the Law He went into hell. In our account, moreover, 3rdly, His shamelessness has an impure region for its sphere of action, and according to the Talmud from

Talmud we have before us in contradistinction to the Babylonian the simpler, because primary, form of the tradition." F. Weber, *System der altsynago- galen paläst. Theologie*, p. xxvii f.

[1] See p. 15*, xv.

[2] See however such passages as Matt. xxiii. 15—36. [A. W. S.]

[3] See p. 17*, xxi. (a).

His very birth onwards He was most intimately connected with
such. Also Jesus' intercourse with the holy women, as well as
also with women who were "sinners" (see John viii. 11) was doubtless remarked by His enemies, and later apparently came to be so
interpreted, as though He had had pleasure in casting glances at
the other sex[1]. 4thly, that according to our passage Jesus was
excommunicated (and in how marvellous a way!) could be no
startling news to his Jewish opponents, just as e.g. the foes of
Luther, had it been possible that any one should come from hell
with the announcement, Luther is sitting in hell, would not in
truth be surprised but would say: Of that we are already aware
The same applies, 5thly, to the statement that the disciple could
no more repent, but had incurred eternal damnation (cp. *Gittin*
57 a). Lastly, the circumstance that the excommunicated person
was the disciple of a Rabbi did not, at least at all times, exclude
the reference to Jesus. When we regard the great lack of Talmudic accounts of Jesus (for they would not concern themselves
with the Gospel ones) it is quite conceivable that they realised
the need of· such and sought to satisfy it, and proceeded to refer
to Jesus this account, which they found appropriate for Him.
At the same time one feature in it certainly was overlooked,
which spoke against the identity of the disciple with Jesus.
That is to say, according to *Shabbath* 104 b[2], Jesus had brought
the art of sorcery with Him out of Egypt. Thus long before
the arrival at the inn He had mentally apostatized. How then
could the excommunication on account of a much slighter offence
in comparison with his sin of sorcery, so trouble Him that He
daily entreated the Rabbi to take Him back? Jesus the sorcerer
would never have done this.

The mistake in the chronology, in conjunction with the fact,
that Jesus could be taken for the disciple of a Rabbi, perhaps
allows of an answer to the question, when was the anonymous
story altered to a story about Jesus? Probably this took place

---

[1] For the strong views expressed by the Talmud on this matter, see Jer.
Kallah 58 c; Bab. *B'rachoth* 61 a.

[2] See p. 5*, I. (a).

before Jesus and R. Aḳiba came to be considered contemporaries (cp. p. 19 above); in any case no Jewish doctor of the
Law can have confused the time of Joshua ben P'rachyah
and that of R. Aḳiba. It will have been a time, in which
different views as to the person of Jesus were promiscuously
circulated, and in which, beside such as saw in Jesus nothing else
than a bastard, there were also those by whom He was quite
confidently reckoned as impious, but nevertheless also as a learned
person, a time, in which the Jews had still intercourse with the
Christians and carried on religious discussions with them. In
these discussions the Christians appealed to the authority of
Jesus, and this made a twofold impression upon the Jews. "He
is a fool," said the one party (*Shabbath* 104 b), just as in the
Gospels the Jews said of Him, "He hath a devil and is mad[1]."
Others on the contrary bestowed applause upon this or that
saying of Jesus, a fact which is both probable in itself, and
distinctly follows from the instance brought by R. Eliezer (towards
the close of the 1st century A.D.), of whom it is related (*Aboda
Zara* 16 b; see below, p. 60)[2] that he approved a saying of Jesus.
(Later indeed he reproached himself bitterly for this agreement.)
To this very day Jesus is described by the Jews as zāḳēn mamrē
[a wrong-headed learned man], and the view is a prevalent one
that He had doctors of the law (Hillel is now generally named)
as teachers. This is also the view of the person who introduced
the name of Jesus, and of the Gemara which refers to *Sanhedrin*
43 a. R. Eliezer has denounced Jesus as a sorcerer and therefore
what is said in *Sanh.* 107 b in like manner relates to Jesus. It
is R. Eliezer, in whose mouth the Talmud puts the assertion
that Jesus had been in Egypt, and had brought thence sorceries
(*Shabbath* 104 b; cp. p. 46). Might we venture to conclude that
he has directly or indirectly been the occasion that by the scholar
of Joshua ben P'rachyah Jesus was understood?

B. *The sorcerer Jesus.* A subject of great weight for Christian Apologetics will now occupy us, the treatment of Jesus'
miracles on the part of the Jews of early time. Far from

[1] John x. 20.　　　　　[2] See p. 13*, XIII. (a).

denying them, the Talmud on the contrary readily admits them, referring them however to Satanic arts. How then can the old and the new rationalists fail to be dumbfounded, if it is objected to them :—See then, the most bitter enemies of Jesus have from the very commencement (cp. Matt. ix. 34) in no wise denied the reality of His miracles, but were from time to time convinced by them, and have transmitted this their conviction by means of tradition ? "We have seen with our own eyes these miraculous deeds"; so the voice of the Jews is borne to us from the Talmud. Moreover he who is inclined to bestow no credence upon this testimony of the enemies of Jesus, he who believes that the sharply observant gaze of these foes may have been mistaken, is beyond the reach of argument. The determination not to believe, has thrown such men's minds into fetters, *Shabbath* 104 b[1]. "There is a tradition; Rabbi Eliezer said to the wise men, Has not the son of Stada brought magic spells from Egypt in an incision on his body [his skin]? They answered him, He was a fool, and we do not take proofs from fools."

The hatred towards Jesus, revealing itself here in the designation Ben Stada, shews that the discussion is to be placed in the latter part of Rabbi Eliezer's life (see pp. 45, 60).

To make this clear the Tosephta, *Shabbath*, XI. (XII.)[2] towards the end (ed. Zuckermandel, p. 126) must be adduced. There it is said ; " He who upon the Sabbath cuts letters upon his body, is according to the view of R. Eliezer guilty, according to the view of the wise not guilty. R. Eliezer said to the wise ; Ben Stada surely learned sorcery by such writing ['brought from Egypt,' Jerusalem *Shabbath*, XII. fol. 13 d]. They replied to him : Should we in any wise on account of one fool destroy all reasonable men ?"

R. Eliezer thus supports his assertion that no one should cut marks on his body or tattoo himself upon the Sabbath, by the fact that Jesus had so done ; the example of this impious one must not be imitated, and especially not upon the Sabbath. The

---

[1] See p. 5*, I. (a).   [2] See p. 10*, IX. (b).

wise men however objected to him that Jesus was a Shoteh [1], and to a person of that kind one does not refer [2].

The assertion that Jesus was a sorcerer, forms the complement of another judgment of the Pharisees as to Jesus' miracles, which is preserved to us in Matt. ix. 34 : " But the Pharisees said, By the prince of the devils casteth he out devils." This judgment was pronounced on a special occasion, namely *à propos* of the casting out of devils. How the Pharisees commonly looked upon and discussed the miracles of Jesus, we may well venture to conclude from the sentence of the Talmud now under our notice, " Jesus wrought his miracles by means of sorcery, which he had brought with him from Egypt." Also the addition "brought with him from Egypt" we may without hesitation look upon as original. For, having regard to the temper of mind of the Pharisees, which made it impossible for them with calm attention to examine Jesus' words and deeds, we may assume it to be absolutely certain, that even at the time of His public ministry they had not once sought credible information at a really well-informed source with regard to the history of His earlier life; but the incomplete and not always trustworthy communications, which they from time to time obtained, according to their view indicated a connexion between Jesus' sojourn in Egypt and the art of sorcery attributed to Him. Only the further addition that the conveyance of the sorcery was effected by means of "an incision which he had made in his flesh," is to be ascribed to a later time, when men dwelt in thought upon the original conception and added to it.

With reference to the miracles of Jesus the Pharisees and doctors of the Law would certainly, had it been possible, either

[1] Fool.

[2] In *Shabbath* 104 b, the question is whether tattooing is writing and so forbidden on the Sabbath. R. Eliezer decides that it is a writing, and appeals to the fact that Ben Stada had employed tattooing for writing purposes. This however the majority decides to be something so extraordinary and foolish, that one has no right on that account to include tattooing under the notion of writing. [G. D.]

have availed themselves of a simple denial or have denounced
them as lies and frauds.   But in the face of the fact that the
miracles took place in the presence of the multitude, that those
who were healed by Christ, for example, the raised Lazarus,
went about through every quarter as living witnesses of the
miraculous power of Jesus; in the face of the fact that His
miracles, much more than His teaching, procured for Him from
time to time that unprecedented amount of support, which
threatened the *status* of the collective priesthood; in the face
moreover of the bewildering impression, which even the Pharisees
could not resist at the sight of His miracles, it was utterly
impossible to ignore these miracles, or to tell the people that all
was cheating.   But their hatred found another expression, which
was fitted to destroy the divine lustre that spread itself around
the Worker of the miracles.   Jesus, they said, is a sorcerer, who
has brought his sorceries from Egypt.

The addition "from Egypt" gives expression to the thought
that Jesus was possessed of a sorcery beyond the common.   Of
Egypt, that land of magic arts, in which they understood how to
imitate the miracles of Moses, it is said in *Ḳiddushin* 49 b:
"Ten measures of sorcery came down into the world.   Egypt
received nine measures, and all the rest of the world one."   We
must lay hold of the distinction which is made in this passage between Egyptian (i.e. intensified), and non-Egyptian (i.e. ordinary)
sorcery, in order to grasp the reason that the Talmud makes
Jesus to have learned this magical art in Egypt, while outside
Egypt magic was nevertheless not altogether strange.   We have
only to compare *Sanhedrin* 45 b, where it is related that
Simeon ben Shetach (member of the Sanhedrin from 79 to
70 B.C.[1]) condemned eighty sorceresses to death; and also the
Mishnah of *Sota*, IX. 13, "unchastity and sorcery have ruined
all"; moreover the lament of Simeon ben Jochai, a teacher
of the 2nd century[2], in *Erubin* 64 b: "The daughters of

---

[1] But his date cannot be precisely determined.   Herzfeld (*Gesch.* II. 140)
gives it as B.C. 90.   [A. W. S.]

[2] He was a pupil of Aḳiba.   [A. W. S.]

Israel are degenerate through sorcery;" lastly, Acts xix. 19,
"And not a few of them that practised curious [magical] arts
brought their books [books of magic] together and burned them
in the sight of all." Nay, the Talmud actually maintains that
no one could be a member of the Sanhedrin, who was not
acquainted with magic; for so it is said in *Sanhedrin*, 17 a, and
Menachoth, 65 a, " None others are brought into the Sanhedrin
save those wise and acquainted with magic" (namely, as Rashi
explains, in order that they might be in a position to expose the
sorcerers, who by their sorcery perverted and misled the people).
Thus the assertion that Jesus had learned his magic arts (not
from native magicians, but) in Egypt, marks him as an arch-
magician. And thus we have once again a forcible confirmation
from a hostile mouth of the extraordinary miraculous powers of
Jesus.

At the base of the Talmudic conception, that Egypt was the
home of specially powerful magic, there is the idea that it was
somehow impossible to fetch the Egyptian magic out of that
country, and so to spread it through the rest of the world. In
illustration of this we shall venture to treat the explanation of
Rashi as connected with an early belief, that "the Egyptian
magicians searched every one who quitted the land of Egypt,
whether he was taking any books of magic with him, in order
that the magical art [namely, the Egyptian] might not come
into other countries." If then Jesus nevertheless succeeded in
bringing Egyptian magic out of Egypt, He could only have
effected it by means of a stratagem. In what did this consist?
In "an incision in his flesh," i.e. he inserted in His flesh
Egyptian magic formulæ.

Of what kind however the magical works of Jesus were, the
Talmud nowhere informs us. But since we read in other passages of the Talmud that the disciples of Jesus performed
miracles of healing in the name of Jesus ben Pandēra, we may
venture to assume that those Jews, who proposed to themselves
the question about the character of the magical works of Jesus,
understood thereby just such works of healing as the disciples

had been able to learn simply from their Master. But this does not exclude the possibility that they had also in mind other magical works of every kind; for the Master has more power than the disciple.

C. *Jesus' teaching.* Two questions have here to be discussed. (1) What is handed down to us in the Talmud as to Jesus' teaching in detail? (2) What charge does the Talmud bring against Jesus' teaching? The character of the expressions used makes it appear expedient to answer the second question first.

The judgment concerning Jesus' teaching has found a threefold expression in the Talmud. In *Shabbath*, 104 b, Jesus, as we saw (p. 45), is called a fool. This designation is given to Jesus partly on account of the teaching which He delivered concerning Himself, that He was the Son of God, or God Himself. This appears from the Jerusalem *Ta'anith*, 65 b[1], where in reference to Numb. xxiii. 19 it is said: "R. Abbahu[2] has said: If a man says to thee 'I am God,' he lies; 'I am Son of Man,' he shall rue it; 'I ascend to heaven,' this holds good of him, 'He has said it and will not effect it.'" This passage alludes to Jesus too clearly to need a word of proof. If any say that He is God and at the same time designate Himself as Son of Man—and this no man save Jesus has ever done—he lies, as R. Abbahu taught; or, to express it more strongly, he is a fool. For the promised proof of the Ascension He is simply unable to bring.

The import of the testimony of Jesus to Himself here spoken of is mentioned also in the following passage from P'sikta Rabbathi (ed. Friedmann, 1880), fol. 100 b f.[3] "R. Chia bar Abba[4] said: 'If the son of the whore saith to thee, There be two

---

[1] See p. 10*, x (a).

[2] Of Cæsarea; a 3rd century teacher. [A. W. S.]

[3] See p. 11*, x (c).

[4] More fully, Chia Rabbah, son of Abba Sela. He flourished about A.D. 216, and was pupil of Rabbi (=Jehudah ben Simon III.), to whom is ascribed the original compilation of the Mishnah. [A. W. S.]

Gods, answer him, I am He of the sea, I am He of Sinai.'
(That is to say, at the Red Sea God appeared to Israel as a
youthful warrior, upon Sinai as an old man, as beseems a law-
giver; but both are one). R. Chia bar Abba said: 'If the son
of the whore say to thee, There be two Gods, answer him, It
is here (Deut. v. 4) written not *Gods* but *the Lord* hath spoken
with you face to face.'"

That God has a son, and that for this reason there are two
Gods, passes here for the teaching of the whore's son, wherein
the reference is clear. From the Scriptures of the Old Testament the Jew is bidden to draw the counter-proof, which indeed
naturally is not adduced as opposed to the testimony actually
borne by Jesus Himself, but only to that of His adherents, who
rest their faith upon Him. Since what R. Chia considers to be
a counter-proof is utterly frivolous, it is clear that it is silly, nay,
ridiculous, to set forth to the world things so illogical and
preposterous.

That Jesus was an idolater; this is the Talmud's second
charge against Jesus' teaching.

Accordingly in the Tractate, which makes the most frequent
mention of Jesus, *Sanhedrin*, 103 a[1], we read the following:
"'Neither shall any plague come nigh thy tent' (Ps. xci. 10), i.e.
thou shalt have no son or disciple who burns his food publicly,
as Jesus the Nazarene;" with which we may compare *B'rachoth*,
17 b; "'In our streets [let there be no breaking]' (Ps. cxliv. 14),
i.e. that we may have no son or disciple, who burns his food
publicly, as Jesus the Nazarene."

With reference to the explanation of the figurative expression
"to burn his food publicly" no absolute *consensus* prevails.
Jacob Levy, the learned editor of the *Neuhebr. Wörterbuch*, gives
two explanations, which contradict one another. He says (II. 272,
s.v. *Jeshu*) "a figurative expression for *apostasy*;" on the contrary (IV. 246, s.v. *Kalach*) "figurative for *to lead a bad life*, to act
contrary to one's teaching." The latter explanation is palpably

---

[1] See p. 11*, XI (a).

false; for never has a Jew said of Jesus, that He taught rightly, but that His life was contrary to His teaching. But the simple fact that He had introduced a new doctrine, which was not the doctrine of the Pharisees, was that which from the commencement and onwards was made a reproach against Him. Levy's first explanation may be considered as holding good so far as that it excusably generalises the special signification. So too Lightfoot and Buxtorf. The former[1] remarks on Luke xxiii. 3 : "To destroy one's food publicly, means with the Talmudists to destroy true doctrine through heresy, the true worship of God through idolatry." And Buxtorf says (*Lex. Rabb.* s.v. *Kadach*), "The figure of speech signifies : to turn aside from the right way, to degenerate, to destroy doctrine, to fall away into heresy and idolatry, and publicly to disseminate and advocate such." The dictionary *Aruch*[2] explains more simply in connexion with *B'rachoth*, 17 b, "[Jesus,] who set up idols in the streets and public places." Here however the idea of burning is not dealt with. Therefore we say, public burning of food is a contemptuous expression for the public offering of sacrifice to idols. That the Christians in their assemblies offered sacrifices to idols, was as firmly the opinion of the Jews of old time, as it is that of many at the present day. Naturally therefore it was concluded that Jesus must have commenced it.

Idolatry is the highest degree of falling away from God. The Talmudic view of Jesus as having fallen away from God and of His apostate teaching has acquired a more general expression in a form which became stereotyped. We mean the saying in *Sanhedrin*, 43 a and 107 b: "Jesus practised sorcery, and corrupted and seduced Israel." In what direction did He corrupt and seduce them ? In that of falling away from the true God and His law to false doctrine and idolatry. And indeed He did it with great success; for His adherents consisted not of a few, but of many, since it is said; "He misled Israel."

---

[1] *Horae Hebraicae et Talmudicae*, in loc.

[2] See Kohut's *Aruch*, Vienna, 1891, s.v. קדד (durchlöchern). [A. W. S.]

Finally, that Jesus was a seducer of the people is further
expressed by the title Balaam, under which in several passages
we are to understand Jesus. Balaam (i.e. devourer of the
people[1], destroyer of the people), besides that he pronounced,
unwillingly indeed, and compelled by the hand of the Lord, the
loftiest divine blessings upon the people of Israel, has inherited
a name through his attempt to lead Israel astray to take part in
impure idolatry. He has therefore received in the Targums[2] the
permanent nickname *rashshi'a*, and passes accordingly for the
type of those impious persons, whose aim is, spiritually or physi-
cally to destroy Israel as a people. Also in a physical sense, we
say, the typical Balaam performs his part as a destroyer of
the people; for so says the Targumist on 1 Chron. i. 43:
"Balaam, the son of Beor, the offender, that is, Laban the
Syrian[3], who joined himself with the sons of Esau and wished
to destroy Jacob and his children." But above all it is the
spiritual destruction of Israel, which is expressed by the symbolic
Balaam, and as such a spiritual destroyer of Israel, Jesus came to
receive the name Balaam. He made a split in the synagogue,
which continues to this hour, and according to the Jewish conception is the greatest destroyer of the people, who has ever
risen up in the midst of Israel; to which we may add further
the comparison with Balaam as a magician. For according to
the Talmudic conception (*Sanhedrin*, 105 a) Balaam was also a
magician of the most loathsome kind, whose doom in hell, according to *Gittin*, 57 a[4], is in accordance with his deserts. Jesus
is the Balaam *par excellence*, the figure who is the historical
fulfilment of the typical Balaam of the Old Covenant.

But it is now necessary to shew in detail that there are
really in the Talmud passages in which Balaam denotes Jesus.
We commence with Mishnah of *Sanhedrin*, x. 2[5]; "Three kings

[1] בלע עם.
[2] And in *Pirke Aboth*, v. 22. [A. W. S.]
[3] Syria=Aram. See Numb. xxiii. 7. [A. W. S.]
[4] See p. 17*, xxi (a).
[5] See p. 12*, xii (a).

and four private persons have no portion in the world to
come. Three kings, namely Jeroboam, Ahab, and Manasseh.
R. Jehudah says: 'Manasseh has a portion therein, for it is said
(2 Chron. xxxiii. 13), And he prayed unto him; and he was
intreated of him, and heard his supplication, and brought him
again to Jerusalem into his kingdom.' It was objected to him,
He brought him again into his kingdom, but He did not bring
him again into the life of the future world. Four private persons,
namely Balaam, Doeg, Ahithophel, and Gehazi." This passage
belongs to the celebrated section, named after its opening word
Chelek[1], which, having first remarked that all Israel has a share in
the future life, specifies the exceptions. Under the head of
these exceptions stand those now adduced. First, three kings.
The cardinal sin common to all three, and so the common cause
of their exclusion from the world to come, consists in this, that
they made the children of Israel to sin by leading them astray
into terrible idolatry, into a total declension from the God of
Israel. The immediate annexing of the four private persons
arouses the conjecture, before one reads their names, that in
their case also the matter has to do with the like sin. And indeed we expect at the head of all the name of Jesus, as the one
who surpassed the three kings in the way of seduction, whom
no one whatever approaches in this sin. We expect Jesus to be
mentioned as the first among the four private persons, who
forfeit the world to come; for we are told in *Gittin*, 57 a, (see
the third main division of our work) that He has in a very
special manner to endure the pains of hell. But our expectation
is, at least apparently, frustrated; we do not find the name of
Jesus. If we were disposed to say, that some reason or other,
now no longer discoverable, presented itself for passing over
Jesus, not only would this be an improbable way out of the
difficulty (for in other respects Jesus is not a person, who is to
be passed over in silence; and in particular, the passage from
Gittin convincingly refutes this way of escape), but we are
straightway prepared for Jesus by the commencement of the

[1] Part, share.

chapter in *Chelek*, which quite unmistakably designates the Christians, as such persons as have no part in the world to come. The words are these: " R. Aḳiba says; He also has no part in the world to come, who reads foreign books, and who whispers over a wound and says: 'I will lay upon thee no sickness, which I have laid upon Egypt, for I am the Lord, thy physician.'" Among the foreign, i.e. not accepted, books are, according to the Gemara upon this passage (fol. 100 b), specially to be understood *Siphrē Minin*, the books of the Judaeo-Christians[1], and the words "who whispers over a wound" refer to the miraculous cures of the Christians. How amazed we are therefore, at the very place where we expect to find a mention of Jesus, to find the name of the non-Israelite Balaam, while yet the chapter is dealing solely with Israel, since all non-Jews according to the view of many Rabbis are as such excluded from a portion in the world to come[2]. It cannot be pleaded that in this chapter there are also non-Jews mentioned besides, namely, the men of pre-Mosaic times. For those after all do not stand outside the Jewish line, but are reckoned as ancestors of Israel. No; inasmuch as the Edomite Doeg must at least in a certain sense be numbered among the Israelites, Balaam is in fact the sole non-Jew, who is introduced among the Israelites failing to attain to the world to come, and that too in the first place! Thus then the following conclusion necessarily presents itself. Since Jesus is not mentioned, and yet cannot be absent; since the Balaam of history, as being a non-Israelite, cannot be intended, so by Balaam we are to understand the symbolic Israelitish Balaam; since in connexion with the three kings who seduce to idolatry and declension, there can be intended only such a Balaam, as incurred the guilt of a like sin with those, and since in this sense Jesus was to the fullest extent Balaam; therefore Balaam here is none other than Jesus, who misled and seduced Israel and made it to sin. This con-

---

[1] But see note on p. 32.
[2] Cp. Weber, *System der altsynagogalen paläst. Theologie*, p. 372.

clusion is confirmed by the three following names, Doeg, Ahithophel, and Gehazi. If the three kings and the first of the
private persons, namely Balaam-Jesus, were all in like manner
seducers of Israel in the direction of idolatry and declension,
and for this and no other cause are declared to lack a share
in the life to come, we should accordingly expect that the case
would be in no respect different with the three sinners who now
follow. But we are astonished to find that not only is this not
the case, but that simply Doeg, Ahithophel, and Gehazi, and just
these three, are named, as if in Israelitish history among those
who did not lead Israel away to declension, but sinned otherwise,
there could not be found more, and more grievous, offenders.
Also the converse question presents itself; If among the four
private persons there are found three, who have committed
another sin than that of seduction, how is it to be explained that
this was not also the rule followed in the case of the kings?
Thus it is abundantly clear that in this proposition relating to
the sole persons not having a part in the world to come, it is
entirely the sin of the seduction of Israel to idolatry and
declension which has furnished the standard. Therefore we may
not add the three names Doeg, Ahithophel, and Gehazi, just as
they there stand, to the list of those sole persons, but, they
must, even as Balaam, be fictitious names of such as, like him
and the three kings, seduced Israel to idolatry and declension.
That no Old Testament characters are meant by them, is clear; for
these are never designated in the Talmud under fictitious names;
and in fact there are found in the Old Testament only those
three kings and Balaam besides as persons with regard to whom
the strong consciousness is cherished, that they sinned in a terrible
way by their seduction. On the other hand, we are referred to
New Testament characters as well by the fact that Balaam, i.e.
Jesus, heads the list of the four who are not kings, as also by the
hesitation, which accords with the nature of the case, to designate
them by their right names, a reluctance which was specially
strong, while the war against Jesus was hotly carried on, e.g. in
the time of Aḳiba, in which for Jesus was substituted *Ben*

Stada, or *Ben Pandēra* or *P'loni*[1], or, as we may now add, *Bil'am ha-rasha'* ('Balaam the wicked'). Now eminent Christians have believed that it is most obvious, along with Gust. Rösch[2], to think of the three Apostles, Peter, James, and John, of whom St Paul says in the Epistle to the Galatians (ii. 9) that they are reputed to be pillars of the church. Moreover, the credit, although in a very perverse way, of having given the first impulse towards understanding Ahithophel as a Christian personage, is due to an Israelite, viz. J. E. Löwy[3].

It might surprise us that in the passage, *Sanh.* 106 b (end)[4], Gehazi, the third of those said above to be excluded from a share in the future world, is absent (see below). But in reality this absence furnishes evidence for the weighty character of our assumption that under Gehazi is to be understood one of the chief apostles. For the Gemara, *Sanhedrin*, 107 b, says of him: "Elisha went to Damascus—for what did he go? R. Jochanan has said, that he went for the conversion of Gehazi. But he was not converted. Elisha said to him: Be converted! He answered him: Is it thus that I am converted by thee? From him that sinneth and maketh the people to sin the possibility of repentance is taken away." There is certainly none of our readers who is not at once struck by the words, with which Gehazi here expresses his inability to repent. For precisely the same words were spoken above (p. 41) by Jesus to His teacher Joshua ben P'rachya. This circumstance of itself shews that here the historical Gehazi changes to the part of the symbolical, and on the other hand the severance of our Gehazi from the two others, Doeg and Ahithophel, utterly surprising, as far as the history is concerned, now has a clear light thrown upon it. For it is a matter of history, and may quite easily have come to the ears of the Jews, that Doeg (Peter) and Ahithophel (James)

---

[1] =Somebody. See Levy, *Neuhebr. Wörterbuch*, iv. 54.

[2] *Theol. Studien u. Kritiken*, 1878, pp. 516—521.

[3] *Kritisch-talmudisches Lexikon*, i. Vienna, 1883, Art. *Ahithophel*.

[4] See p. 12*, XII (d).

were prematurely[1] deprived by violence of their lives. In the
same way it is a matter of history that Gehazi (John) was not
executed, but lived on, namely, according to the Jewish view, in
his obstinacy and inability to be converted.

After we have thus obtained from the Mishnah of *Sanhedrin*, x. the evidence for the name Balaam being used as a
designation of Jesus, it is not difficult for us in the following
Balaam-passage also to recognise a Jesus-passage, which on its
part again serves to throw light on *Sanhedrin*, x. 2. In *Aboth*,
v. 19[2], the disciples of " Balaam the wicked " are named in opposition to the disciples of our father Abraham, and the following
distinction is offered between the two; "The disciples of our
father Abraham enjoy this world and inherit the world to come,
as it is written (Prov. viii. 21), 'That I may cause those that love
me to inherit substance, and that I may fill their treasuries:'
the disciples of Balaam the impious inherit Gehenna, and go
down into the pit of destruction, as it is written (Ps. lv. 24):
'But thou, O God, shalt bring them down into the pit of
destruction: bloodthirsty and deceitful men shall not live out
half their days.'" This passage deals, as we see, with the
division of the Jews into two halves, and with the absolute
opposition of the two halves, parting into heaven and hell.
Abraham's disciples, or, as the Jews[3] proudly call themselves,
Abraham's children, are the pious, who after death come into
Abraham's bosom[4], i.e. take up their abode in the genial presence
of their blessed progenitor, who dwells in Paradise. Balaam's
disciples on the other hand are the impious, who go to hell into
endless pain. Who is Balaam in this passage? That the historical
Balaam is thought of, is unlikely, even if we were only considering this passage in itself. Or might we venture to take Jesus for

[1] This adverb applies in strictness to the latter only, St Peter's death
occurring not earlier than A.D. 66—68. See Smith's *Dict. of Bible*, Art.
Peter. [A. W. S.]

[2] See p. 12*, xii (b).

[3] Cp. John viii.

[4] Luke xvi. 22.

one of the disciples of Balaam, and say that He is included among these? This would mean, to moderate the burning hatred felt against Jesus so as to place him on a level with all other reprobates. If we take cognizance further of the fact that in *Sanhedrin*, x. 2, Balaam (i.e. Jesus), when taken strictly, is specified as the only one of the four private persons who go bereft of the future life (for the three others represent only His disciples), it becomes quite clear that in the same way in chap. v. of the Treatise *Aboth*, Balaam, the father and master of those who go astray, is none other than Jesus. We may bear in mind also the Old Testament passage referring to the deceitful men who do not live out half their days. And this introduces us to another Balaam-passage.

In *Sanhedrin*, 106 b[1], we read "A Jewish Christian (*Min*[2]) said to R. Chanina: Hast thou by any chance ascertained, what age Balaam was? He answered: There is nothing written concerning it. But since it is said, 'Bloodthirsty and deceitful men shall not live out half their days,' he was either 33 or 34 years old. The Jewish Christian answered, Thou hast spoken well; for I have myself seen a chronicle of Balaam, in which it is said: Thirty-three years old was Balaam the lame man, when the robber Phinehas slew him." Further we take another passage from *Sanhedrin*, 106 b, (end)[3] "R. Jôchanan said: Doeg and Ahithophel lived not half their days. Such too is the tenor of a Boraitha: Bloodthirsty and deceitful men shall not live out half their days. All the years of Doeg were not more than thirty-four, and of Ahithophel not more than thirty-three." Further if we admit that the short lifetime of Balaam, Doeg, and Ahithophel was invented to the end that they might be represented as reprobates, still the almost absolute identity of the figures strikes us. This points on the one side to that combination, in which the names stand side by side in the Mishnah of *Sanhedrin*, x., and now on the other side the number thirty-three (thirty-four) confirms the view that there, as here, under Balaam

---

[1] See p. 12*, xii (c).   [2] But see note on p. 32.
[3] See p. 12*, xii (d).

is to be understood Jesus.   For it is well-known with regard to
Jesus that He lived thirty-three to thirty-four years (cp. Luke
iii. 23), an abbreviation of the duration of life, which,. we may
easily perceive, must have excited the Jews to a comment of the
above-mentioned kind.   After His model then Doeg and Ahithophel have had allotted to them a like duration of life, especially
since it was known of them that they[1], like Jesus, did not in fact
fill up the measure of their days, but like Him were forcibly
removed from life before their time.   The way in which this
forcible removal is related is now the other feature of the story,
which points to Jesus.   A "chronicle of Balaam," which the
Christian knew and which R. Chanina had not read, was simply
the New Testament.   That Phinehas cannot have been the son
of Eleazar, the son of Aaron, mentioned in Numb. xxv. 2 ff.,
who at Moses' command led an army against the Midianites,
and slew their kings together with Balaam with the sword, is
clear from the epithet *Lista'a*[2], "the robber."   In reality the
Christian said something of this kind to R. Chanina : Jesus was
thirty-three years of age, when Pontius Pilate slew him.   Pontius
Pilate—this man, as the Targum Sheni on the Book of Esther
shews, has never been forgotten by the Jews.   Had he then, he
who even apart from this dealt out only evil against the Jews[3],
he, who belonged to the hated Roman race,—had he almost
rescued from the Jews their prey, Jesus ! Is it not natural that
the Jewish passion for caricature, especially where fictitious
names (Balaam, Doeg, Ahithophel, Gehazi) had been already
employed, should have set itself to work upon this name also ?
Lista'a cannot with Rashi be explained General (*Sar tzaba*),
but is a mutilated form of *P'lista'a*[4].   Since Jesus was indicated

---

[1] I have been unable to find any tradition outside the Talmud with regard
to the death of Doeg. [A. W. S.]   He is mentioned (commonly together with
Ahithophel) in the following passages, *Sanh.* 69 b, 93 b, 105. *Ber.* 17 b (beg.),
Chag. 15 b, Jeb. 77 a (beg.), Sota 21 a, Zeb. 54 b. [H. L. S.]

[2] $= \lambda\eta\sigma\tau\acute{\eta}\varsigma$.   [3] Cp. Jost, *Geschichte des Judenthums*, i. 333.

[4] Levy, *Neuhebr. Wörterb.* ii. 503 ; cp. also Perles, *Zur rabbinischen Sprach-
und Sagenkunde*, 1873, p. 16.

by " Balaam" (see Numb. xxxi. 6—8), it was natural to call him
who caused the punishment of death to be carried out upon
Him, Phinehas, and indeed the more so, as this name had to
some extent a similar sound to Pontius. Lastly, as regards the
epithet, "the lame man," by which Balaam in our passage is
designated, Levy (I. 236) says thus, that according to Jewish
tradition 'Jesus became lame, inasmuch as he had been forcibly
deprived of a charm, in consequence of which he had fallen
down from a height.' But this tradition was probably first
devised in connexion with the epithet "the lame man," which it
was invented to explain. The occasion for the term of contempt
"the lame man" we find in the history of the sufferings of
Jesus, whether it be in His breaking down under the load of the
Cross ("He who helped the palsied to walk has become lame,
and cannot raise himself to his feet!"), or whether it be in the
piercing of His feet when they were nailed to the Cross.

Lastly, we adduce further a Balaam-passage which, in a very
special way, renders it manifest, how much the historical Balaam
was viewed with a side reference to the symbolic Balaam, Jesus.
In *Sanhedrin*, 106 a[1], it is said with reference to Numb. xxiv. 23[2],
which gives a remark of Balaam : Resh Laḳish has said ; "Woe
to him who recalls himself to life by the name of God." This
sense, or rather perversion, of the words of Balaam points to
Jesus too obviously for a proof to be needed. For of whom
would it ever have been said, that he had recalled himself to
life ? Rashi explains, "Balaam, who recalled himself to life by
the name of God, made himself thereby to be God." Rashi, of
course, did not believe in the Resurrection of Jesus, but he means
that it would be a piece of madness, if a man should make himself out to be God, and support this by the doctrine proclaimed
by his adherents, that he had raised himself from the dead by
means of the name of God. In Midrash *Tanchuma*, Parasha
Mattoth[3], it is related that Balaam along with the kings of Midian

[1] See p. 13*, XII (e).
[2] "Alas, who shall live when God doeth this?" [A. W. S.]
[3] Ed. Mantua, 1563, fol. 91c; not in the part published by Buber.

flew through the air, but was precipitated to the ground by the name of God on the forehead-plate of the high priest. There may be an allusion to this in *Sanhedrin*, 106 a. In that case it is to be rendered : "Woe to him who seeks to preserve his life by the name of God, applied with magical arts." With this Balaam-passage, with which the Palestinian *Ta'anith* 65 (see above, p. 50) is to be compared, we close our proof that Jesus is called Balaam, a name which combines the imputations brought against Jesus in the Talmud, *Sanhedrin*, 43 a, namely sorcery and the seduction of Israel to idolatry and declension.

After we have thus learned to know the judgment of the Talmud as to Jesus' teaching, which amounted to this, that He was charged with folly, idolatry, and seduction of the people, we turn now to the two sentences which are handed down in the Talmud expressly as sayings of Jesus.

Aboda zara, 16 b, 17 a[1]: The Rabbis have handed down the following : When R. Eliezer[2] was about to be imprisoned on account of heresy [*Minuth*, a leaning towards the forbidden Christian religion], he was brought to the [Roman] court of justice to be tried. The judge said to him : Does a man of mature years like thee busy himself with such nullities ? Eliezer replied ; The Judge is just towards me. The judge thought that Eliezer was speaking of him ; but he thought upon his Father in heaven. Then spake the judge: Since I believe thee[3], thou art acquitted[4]. Now when Eliezer came home, his disciples presented themselves to console him, but he admitted no consolation. Then R. Akiba

[1] See p. 13*, xiii (a).

[2] Eliezer ben Hyrkanus, the famous pupil of Jochanan ben Zakkai, and teacher of Akiba. He founded a school at Lod (=Lydda, cp. 1 Chr. viii. 12 ; Acts ix. 32), later called Diospolis, near Joppa. Lod was also a very important Jewish tribunal. See p. 213, and for interesting details see Neubauer, *Géog. du Talmud*, pp. 76 ff. [A. W. S.]

[3] Rather, Since I am held by thee to be just. [G. D.]

[4] Or, more fully, I swear to thee that thou etc. However, the sense of the expression rendered "I swear to thee" is disputed. Perhaps דימוס is the Greek δεῖμα, fear, and refers to his god (for the expression cp. Gen. xxxi. 42, 53), or his tutelary deity. [A. W. S.]

said to him : Permit me to tell thee something of what thou hast
taught me. He answered : Say on. Then said R. Aḳiba : Perchance thou hast once given ear to a heresy, which pleased thee ;
on account of which thou wast now about to be imprisoned for
heresy. Eliezer replied : Aḳiba, thou remindest me. I was once
walking in the upper street of Sepphoris[1] ; there I met with one
of the disciples of Jesus the Nazarene, by name Jacob of K'phar
S'khanya[2] who said to me : It is found in your law (Deut. xxiii.
19[3]) "Thou shalt not bring the hire of a whore...into the house
of...thy God." May a retiring place for the high-priest be made
out of such gifts? I knew not what to answer him to this.
Then he said to me : Thus Jesus of Nazareth taught me : "Of
the hire of an harlot hath she gathered them, and unto the hire
of an harlot shall they return" (Mic. i. 7). From offal it has
come ; to the place of offal shall it go. This explanation pleased
me, and on this account have I been impeached for heresy, because
I transgressed the Scripture : "Remove thy way far from her"
(Prov. v. 8), from her, i.e. from heresy.

At the first reading it may be doubted whether a saying of
Jesus can be really presented here, for we are accustomed to see
Jesus come forward in word or deed only in these significant
occasions, which the Evangelists have selected and recorded out
of the immeasurably rich treasure of His sayings and acts. But
Jesus surely often had occasion also to answer unimportant
questions of His disciples or of the Pharisees. Accordingly we
have not to ask, whether a saying of Jesus furnished us in the
Talmud or elsewhere is equally important with those laid up in the
sacred records, but whether it is unworthy of Jesus or not. And
from this point of view there is nothing to be said against the
alleged originality of our saying.

Further, it were to be desired that the Talmud had informed
us, by whom Jesus had been asked the question, whether by a

[1] A city in the middle of lower Galilee. See Neubauer, pp. 191—195.
[A. W. S.]

[2] Sikhnin. See Neubauer, pp. 234—5. [A. W. S.]

[3] A.V. and R.V. 18. [A. W. S.]

disciple or a Pharisee ; likewise, whether the question was put to Jesus on the occasion of a particular incident, or, as often occurs in the Talmud, with reference to a fictitious case.   The words " Thus Jesus taught me" appear indeed to suggest that the questioner was no other than the aforesaid Jacob of K'phar S'khanya.   But in the first place it is in no way necessary to press this expression ; for what Jesus taught was said to each of those present ; nay, even absent persons, and even those who lived later, might introduce an expression of Jesus, which they had appropriated to themselves, with the words "Thus Jesus teaches me."   Then as regards the story before us, it is almost impossible that Jacob of K'phar S'khanya had himself asked Jesus and received the answer from Him ; for between the death of R. Eliezer, with whom Jacob here speaks, and the death of Jesus there lie quite eighty years. It may be that the Talmud, which (see above, pp. 22, 37) wrongly places Jesus in the time of Eliezer and Akiba, has the notion, that Jacob had heard the expression direct from the mouth of Jesus.   But this conception is not correct ; Jacob had not received the expression otherwise than through tradition.—Then as concerns the other point, whether the question was put to Jesus with reference to an occasion furnished by actual circumstances, or whether it dealt with a purely imaginary case, no definite answer can be given.   The former seems to us the more likely ; it was not till the Talmudic period, in which Temple, sacrifices, and the rest were no longer in existence, that they began to discuss fictitious cases.

The question therefore was, whether the price of a courtesan, which was placed at the disposal of the high-priest for the fitting up of a retiring place to the chamber, where the high-priest had to pass the last week before the Day of Atonement (see Mishnah of *Joma* i. 1), might be appropriated thereto, or whether the precept of Deut. xxiii. 18 is here to be regarded; in other words, whether that retiring place, which confessedly belonged to the Temple-buildings, is holy : a question, which seems to us almost ridiculously trivial, but was by no means such for the Jews of that day.   Therefore Jesus also does not simply repel the ques-

tioner with words of rebuke, but gives him a complete answer,
" How can the retiring place, although belonging to the Temple,
be holy? It is an unclean place. Thus the precept, Deut.
xxiii. 18, does not stand in the way. The application of hire
derived from an impure source to the erection of the retiring
place is not only permitted, but altogether suitable. It comes
from uncleanness. Let it then go to the place of uncleanness, in
accordance with the words of the prophet Micah (i. 7)."

Jesus' manner of grasping the principle of a question, and
answering it more completely than the questioner intended, shews
itself also in this saying. It would indeed have obviously satis-
fied the questioner, if he had been referred by Jesus to Deut. xxiii.
12—14, from which passage it appears clearly enough that a
retiring place has nothing to do with holiness, but brings upon
itself the reverse character. But Jesus, presupposing, it would
appear, this passage as known, gives the questioner this further
instruction, namely, that such hire is adapted in a singularly
suitable way for the fitting up of a retiring place : From offal to
offal. And this teaching He supports by an Old Testament
prophecy, whose figurative expression He employs in the literal
sense : From the hire of a courtesan the money is obtained ; it
shall go back to the hire of a courtesan, i.e. it shall be subjected
to the fate, which is appropriate for such polluted money. At
the bottom of this prophecy there lies the principle of divine
retribution, and this principle in its turn rests upon the divine
maxim, that things which belong to each other shall come
together, just as on the other hand it is a divine maxim,
that things which do not belong to one another should remain
severed from one another, and not be mingled together (cp.
especially Lev. xix. 19 ; Deut. xxii. 5); for God is a God of
order.

Jacob of K'phar S'khanya was manifestly seeking to bring R.
Eliezer nearer to Christianity, and opened the conversation at a
point where, as he was persuaded, he must elicit a concession from
the Rabbi. Accordingly he laid himself out in the first place to
prove to R. Eliezer that Jesus was eminently learned in the Law.

S.   5

And—he succeeded : Eliezer was not only himself pleased [1] with
the decision of Jesus, but actually extended it further. When
Eliezer after the expiration of a long time was arraigned for
heresy and could discover no cause for it, R. Aḳiba reminded him
of that day on which he had spoken with Jacob of K'phar
S'khanya, and had accepted the saying of Jesus imparted by him.
Hence it is seen that that was the sole occasion that R. Eliezer
had drawn a little nearer to the teaching of Jesus. And what
issues had this one occasion had for him! It had called forth a
storm which had prevented him from occupying himself further
with Jesus' teaching, so that the little seed scattered by Jacob
was blighted in the germ.

To understand the excitement, which Eliezer's approval of a
saying of Jesus evoked, it is by no means necessary to examine
wherein exactly the heresy of the saying lay. That it originated
from Jesus was ground enough to condemn it as heretical. What
good thing can come from Jesus?—such was the purport of an
Aḳiba's views—even that which is good, only appears so, and has
a corrupting influence, because behind it there lies an apostate
mind. Jewish fanaticism asked not then, and asks not even at
the present day: Is what is said true or false? but: Who has
said it? and sentence is pronounced accordingly.

The other saying of Jesus handed down by the Talmud we
find in *Shabbath* 116 a and b[2]: Imma Shalom, the wife of R.
Eliezer and sister of Rabban[3] Gamaliel [II] had a philosopher as
a neighbour, who had the reputation of taking no bribe. They
wished to render him ridiculous. Imma accordingly brought
him a golden candlestick, presented herself before him, and said:
'I should like to have a share in the property of my family'[4].

[1] Cp. Luke xx. 39.

[2] See p. 14*, xiv.

[3] On the somewhat difficult question, to whom the title Rabban belonged,
I may be permitted to refer to *A Translation of the Treatise Chagigah, etc.*,
Cambridge, 1891, pp. 150, 151, with the authorities there mentioned. [A. W. S.]

[4] Literally, "house of women." She means, the property belonging to
her own side of the house, as a daughter of Simeon ben Gamaliel I., as
opposed to that which was in the possession of her husband's family. [G. D.]

The philosopher answered her: 'Then have thy share!' But Gamaliel said to him: 'We have the law: Where there is a son, the daughter shall inherit naught.' The philosopher said: 'Since the day, when ye were driven out of your country, the Law of Moses is repealed and there is given the Gospel, in which it is said: Son and daughter shall inherit together.' On the next day Gamaliel brought the philosopher a Libyan ass. Then the philosopher said to them: 'I have looked at the end of the Gospel; for it says: I, the Gospel, am not come to do away with the Law of Moses, but to add to the Law of Moses am I come. It is written in the Law of Moses: Where there is a son, the daughter shall not inherit.' Then Imma said to him: 'Nevertheless may thy light shine like the candlestick.' But Rabban Gamaliel said: 'The ass is come and has overturned the candlestick.'

What object these two, Imma and her brother Gamaliel, had, when they addressed themselves to render the "philosopher" ridiculous (by whom we are to understand, according to Rashi, a Jewish Christian, according to Levy [1], a Christian judge) is not told us. But if we observe how much importance they attached to it, inasmuch as they expended no small sum, and if we remember that R. Eliezer, the husband of Imma, and brother-in-law of Gamaliel, was held to be favourably disposed to Christians, we shall scarcely go wrong in assuming that this action on the part of the two was not in the main to turn the Christian into ridicule for its own sake, but in order to rend from him the mask of Christian virtue, and undoubtedly too with a regard to Eliezer. Accordingly Imma sent to the "philosopher" who lived in her neighbourhood a golden candlestick, to influence him in her favour, and then presented herself with her brother before him. The philosopher on account of the golden candlestick decides forthwith in accordance with Imma's desires. To Gamaliel's protest he objects: " From the time that the Jewish nation has been without a country, the Law of Moses is repealed, and replaced by the Gospel, which says that son and daughter

[1] *Neuhebr. Wörterb.* I. 46 b.

inherit alike." On the following day Imma and Gamaliel presented themselves once more before the Christian, after Gamaliel
had previously sent him a Libyan ass. Now the Christian,
altered in his views by the more valuable present, decides as
follows : " I have looked at the end of the Gospel, where it says :
I am not come to do away with the Law of Moses, but to add to
the Law of Moses am I come. Accordingly the Gospel adheres
to that which the Law of Moses says : Where there is a son, the
daughter does not inherit." Thereupon Imma says, alluding to
her candlestick : " May thy light however shine like the candlestick ! " But Gamaliel exclaims : " I have prevailed. My ass has
overturned thy candlestick." And thus the Christian was proved
in the most provoking manner to be accessible to bribery.

The first sentence adduced by the " philosopher " is found
nowhere in the New Testament. It was certainly never spoken
by Jesus, Who Himself maintained the commandments of Moses,
and only relieved them of Rabbinic accretions and distortions.
" The new," says Delitzsch[1], " was not to bring itself into acceptance by a sudden and forcible breaking away from the old, but
by gradually working itself clear from it. And since we may
not assume that the Lord during His sojourn here below subjected Himself to the Mosaic Law only in appearance, or only so
far as it was a calculated means by which He should attain to an
end lying beyond it, so we cannot avoid the conclusion that when
He used that expression ' I am not come to destroy, but to fulfil[2] ',
in His consciousness this spiritual fulfilment of the Law did not
yet admit of doing away with the observance of the ceremonial
Law. It was not till He died that He died to the Law as
restricted to the nation, and it was not till He rose again from
the dead that He was manifest as the End of the Law." Although Jesus thus under no circumstances uttered the saying
"Son and daughter inherit together," yet this saying had from
apostolic times an acceptance with Christians, and it might very

[1] *Saat auf Hoffnung*, 1888, p. 9.
[2] Matt. v. 17.

well be quoted as a saying of the Gospel, if under the word
Gospel there were understood in the wider sense the religion of
the New Covenant, which has stripped off everything Jewish in
the national sense, and has made love the standard of all action.
There is a Gospel saying—so it might be put—that the daughter
should also be given a share in the patrimony. But that under
the word *Gospel*, to which this saying belonged, the "philosopher" desired should be understood, not the religion of the New
Testament generally, but a book, which bore the title "Gospel,"
indisputably follows from his statement the next day that he had
looked at the end of the Gospel (namely, of that, from which he
had taken the first quoted saying), and there had found a saying
of another import. And since this latter saying "I am not come
etc." is plainly a saying taken from Christ's Sermon on the Mount
(Matt. v. 17), the "philosopher" unquestionably wished the
former too to be regarded as a saying of Jesus. He who was
dazzled by Imma's golden candlestick was able the more easily to
make the two Jews believe the utterance of Jesus, albeit historically false and in itself impossible, inasmuch as they to all appearance did not themselves possess the Gospel and also had no desire
to read it. There is no need of a serious investigation, how the
"philosopher" came to assert that he had read the second saying
at the end of the Gospel. Since he lied in regard to the first
saying, so it was also a lie that he had read the other saying in a
later passage, or indeed at the end of the Gospel. It is quite a
question, whether he possessed a text of the Gospels. For let us
proceed to compare the wording in the Talmud with that in the
Gospel. We have absolutely no cause for believing that the
Talmud does not transmit the sentence exactly as the "philosopher" quoted it. Since then the variation from the wording in
the Gospel cannot be referred to an intentional alteration, we
must assume that the "philosopher" simply did not know the
sentence in any other form. He had not borrowed it from a text
of the Gospels, but had drawn it from his defective memory.
And so in this perverted form the sentence has passed over into
the Talmud, whereupon the latter, after its fashion, has not been

able to deny itself the slight alteration of adding to the " I " (i. e.
Jesus) the word in apposition, namely, ' Avōn-Gillayōn, which
word, a parody on *Evangelium*, means " sin-register or writing "
(cp. p. 13); so that now under the " I " the Gospel is to be
understood in opposition to the Law.

How far then—this we have still to ask at the close—do the
two sentences adduced by the " philosopher " supply to the Jew of
the Talmud an explanation of the general charge of folly and
seduction ?   The one sentence—never spoken by Jesus—asserts
that He had set aside a commandment of Moses ; the other that
He had taken nothing from the Law, but rather had added to
it.   Both sentences severally support the charge that Jesus was
an apostate and a seducer to the renouncing of God, and indeed,
so far as He uttered both conjointly, a deceiver.   If they joined
with this the idea, that Jesus in the consciousness of His being the
Son of God, on account of which He was taken for a fool, pronounced the sentence that He was come to add to the Law of
Moses, in this sentence was found the confirmation of His folly.

At the close of this discussion we merely reiterate the fact,
which is indeed eagerly combated by the Jews, that numerous
sentences, which in the Talmud are placed specifically in the
mouth of Jewish authorities, might with greater correctness be
ascribed to Jesus or to the Apostles.   The proof of this lies
beyond the limits of our task, which aims at collecting and illus-
trating the evident testimony of the Talmud with regard to
Jesus [1].

---

[1] It may be permitted however to adduce two judgments of prominent
Christian scholars which bear upon this subject. 1. Franz Delitzsch in his
work, *Was D. August Wohling beschworen hat und beschwören will* (Leipzig,
1883), p. 11, remarks: " I believe that I can shew by convincing historical
proofs, that the preaching of Jesus and of primitive Christianity in its
original Jewish form has been a power, through the working of which
a stream of brightness as it were has diffused itself through Talmudic
literature. No doubt this shews itself more in the structure of the liturgy
and in the more unfettered course of thought in the Haggada than in' the
legal teaching of Halacha, dependent as this was on certain traditional
principles and rules of interpretation." 2. Heinrich Thiersch in his book,

D. JESUS' DISCIPLES. In one passage of the Talmud the
disciples (*Talmidim*) of Jesus are expressly spoken of. What
is found related of these disciples indeed, namely, their crucifixion, as well as the circumstance that this narrative is immediately connected with the account of the Crucifixion of Jesus, are
a sufficient security that the name of disciple was not meant in
the remotest degree to redound to those persons' honour. They
were disciples, but disciples of whom? Of a man, whose end was
crucifixion. They were disciples, and partook of what honour?
That of crucifixion, like their Master. What a disgrace under such
circumstances to be designated by the name "disciple." The story
then of the rabble of disciples—such is the notion of the Talmud
—is worded as follows, *Sanhedrin* 43 a [1]. There is a tradition:
Jesus had five disciples: Mathai (Matthew), Nakkai, Netzer,

Ueber den christlichen Staat (Basel, 1875), p. 236 f., makes the following
remark: "In reference to swearing Christ also found degeneration and
abuses among the Jews. Asseverations by oath were usual in ordinary life,
as is indicated in Matt. v. 33—37, and Jam. v. 12. Untruthfulness in
speech was widespread; and it could not be said of many, as the Lord said
of Nathanael: 'Behold, an Israelite indeed, in whom is no guile!' (Joh. i. 47).
At the same time the Jewish people still had a reverence and awe for the name
of God. Thus there arose the custom, to weave into their daily speech
forms of oath, in which the name of God was avoided. They asseverated
this or that by heaven, by the earth, by Jerusalem, by their own head, and
they were not particular about truth. This evil practice was followed by
a still worse theory, which was to serve as an excuse for the former: 'Whosoever sweareth by the temple, it is nothing, but he that sweareth by the
gold of the temple, he is a debtor. Whosoever sweareth by the altar, it is
nothing, but he that sweareth by the sacrifice that is upon it, he is a debtor.'
Against such distinctions the Lord contended (Matt. xxiii. 16—23); and
from His words in Matt. v. 33—37 we conclude that there were doctors of
the Law who considered, that if only the name of God were not expressly
mentioned, it did not matter much about the truth of the assertion. It
was considered enough, to keep the oath taken to God. We mention it to
the honour of the Jews, that these excuses for lying are not found in the
Talmud. The testimony of Christ against all this has not been in vain."

[1] See p. 15*, xv.; but for translation of the earlier part of the passage,
see below, p. 86.

Bunni, Todah.   Mathai was brought before the judgment seat. He said to the judges : " Is Mathai to be put to death ?   Yet it is written ; ' *Mathai* [= when] shall I come and appear before God ? ' " (Ps. xlii. 3 [1]).   They answered him : " Nay, but Mathai is to be executed : for it is said : ' Mathai [when] shall [he] die and his name perish ? ' " (Ps. xli. 6 [2]).   Nakkai was brought.   He said to them : " Is Nakkai to be put to death ?   Yet it is written : ' The Naki [the innocent] and righteous slay thou not ' " (Ex. xxiii. 7).   They replied to him : " Nay, but Nakkai is to be put to death : for it is written : ' In covert places doth he put to death the Naki ' " (Ps. x. 8).   Netzer was brought.   He said to them : " Is Netzer to be put to death ?   Yet it is written : ' A Netzer [branch] shall spring up out of his roots ' " (Is. xi. 1).   They answered him : " Netzer is to be put to death ; for it is said : ' Thou art cast forth from thy sepulchre, like an abominable Netzer ' " (Is. xiv. 19).   Bunni was brought. He said : " Is Bunni to be put to death ?   Yet it is written : ' Israel is B'ni [my son], my first-born ' " (Ex. iv. 22).   They answered him : " Nay but Bunni is to be put to death ; for it is written : ' Behold, I will slay Binkha [thy son], thy first-born ' " (Ex. iv. 23).   Todah was brought.   He said to them : " Is Todah to be put to death ?   Yet it is written : ' A Psalm for Todah [thanksgiving] ' " (Ps. c. 1, heading).   They answered him : " Nay but Todah is to be put to death : for it is written : 'Whoso offereth Todah honoureth me ' " (Ps. l. 23).

The whole narrative bears the stamp of impossibility on its face.   Or could any one be found actually to believe that men sentenced to death had sought to save themselves by adducing to the judge as objections Old Testament passages, from which in accordance with a Rabbinic interpretation of the text they should be dismissed with their lives ?   If they were once de-clared deserving of death, the death penalty could only be averted by a so-called *Zakhuth* [justifying plea], but never in any case by a punning quotation.   In the same way it is impossible to

---

[1] So Heb. but ver. 2 in A. V. and R. V.   [A. W. S.]

[2] So Heb. but ver. 5 in A. V. and R. V.   [A. W. S.]

suppose, that the judges should have troubled themselves by
means of a like interpretation of a text to furnish a proof that
the Old Testament had already announced by anticipation the
death of those condemned persons. As though at any time a
judge, in presence moreover of a hated and despised defendant,
would have allowed himself a conversation and argument of
the kind. And independently of all this, the Talmud requires
of its readers, to picture to themselves the five, as possessed one
and all with the same notion, that they should simply rid themselves in this preposterous fashion from the death penalty, and as
having either studied their plea beforehand or having hit on it
impromptu when face to face with the judge.

But, although this narrative in the form here presented is
absurd, yet it is not devoid of an historical background. Only
we must not allow the number five, which, as it appears to us, is
nothing but a corruption of the number twelve, to mislead us
into imagining the disciples to be apostles, or in general into
clinging scrupulously to the apostolic age. Otherwise we should
pass from one difficulty into another.

The number five, we say, is an alteration from the number
twelve, no longer recognised, it is true, by the later Talmudists,
who have received the story by tradition, but altogether intentional on the part of its author. For to venture on the assumption that the number five was set down by him quite arbitrarily,
merely for the general purpose of giving *some* number, is not
practicable for this reason, that we can in fact discover no interest
which could induce him to hit arbitrarily upon a definite number,
which moreover had no value except merely that it was a number.
No, the author must plainly have had a peculiar interest in
the number five. But then it is not enough to say that his
motive was to indicate by this number the pitiably small quantity
of disciples possessed by Jesus. The author knew that Jesus had
many adherents ; therefore, if the number of the apostles had
been unknown to him, he would unquestionably have set down a
larger number, certainly not merely five. Accordingly in the
employment of the number five, contemptible through its small-

ness, there must lie a scoff at the sacred number twelve, that of the Apostles [1].

The death by martyrdom of these disciples, related in the Talmud, and in fact in connexion with the execution of Jesus in Lud, opens out to us a fairly clear view of the time in which, and of the circumstances under which, that execution is to be thought of as carried out. If we remember that the Talmud takes no notice of the extremely full Church history belonging to the Talmudic age, that for it this history is absolutely non-existent, we are not disposed, when investigating the time and the immediate circumstances of our story, to pass beyond the limits of the Talmud itself, but we shall be obliged, especially on account of the great animation of the narrative, to take up our position in the age of R. Akiba, of which we have already several times made mention. In that age the hatred of Judaism towards Christianity burned brightly, a hatred, of which, as is already known to our readers, forcible traces have been preserved uneffaced. An execution of Christians is here notified to us. What execution then, what slaying of Christians could more easily be preserved in the memory than those which took place under Bar Koch'ba? (cp. the passage from Justin's *Apology* on p. 15 above). For let us realise the effect which the attacks of Akiba, the famous Rabbi of Lud, had upon the views as to the person of Jesus: the subsequent age took Jesus for his contemporary, who was executed in Lud! In addition there is the circumstance that our narrative is connected with that of the execution of Jesus in Lud, i.e., in the town of Akiba, a thing which of itself is quite sufficient to place the execution of the five disciples of Jesus in the closest relation with Akiba. Another indication too points to the time of Akiba; the circumstance, that it is a Jewish tribunal, by which

[1] The number five might perhaps also have its origin in the five wounds of Jesus. That these wounds, held sacred by the Christians (cp. the hymn: "Wir bitten dich, wahr Mensch u. Gott, durch dein heilig 5 Wunden rot"), were claimed by the Jews as a mark for ridicule, is highly probable. And that their scorn, influenced by an unbridled imagination, made out of the wounds disciples, is not so very farfetched or over-difficult a conception.

the disciples are condemned. For although we must note the alleged citation of proof-texts on either side as unhistorical, thus much in any case is shewn by the narrative, that it was no heathen court of justice, but a Jewish one. This fits in with the period of Bar Koch'ba, the last period of Jewish independence.

After these introductory remarks as to time and circumstances we proceed to judge the narrative with regard to its historical character. It is not really conceivable that without a special inducement the deviser of the proceedings in court took up the idea of carrying out his mocking play upon the names. We find this inducement in the word *Mathai*. In the words of Mathai, whom we take to be an actual Christian of the time of Akiba, in the words " When [Mathai] shall I come and appear before God?" we have the longing prayer of the afflicted one, to be delivered from his torment. This lament was scornfully answered by another saying from the Psalms : " Mathai, his name shall perish." This jeer met with such great applause, that the desire was felt to abuse the names of some more Christians in the same way ; and since it was remembered that Matthew was the name of one of the Twelve, the imaginary history was prefaced by the assertion that they were disciples of Jesus, which may have at once determined their number, namely five in opposition to twelve. If then the deviser of the story scornfully changed the familiar number twelve to that of five, without experiencing opposition, it excites no surprise that he also made use of names, which have nothing to do with the names of the twelve. If we have regard to the fictitious character, which in more than one respect so plainly belongs to the narrative, it is by no means necessary to take the names generally as historical. What the author of the fiction aimed at in fact was not truth but simply mockery. But of course the ridicule was the more pointed, if through the names a parody was introduced upon what was actually Christian or otherwise contemptible in the eyes of the Jews. It is obvious that similarity of sound was enough for the parodies (comp. p. 72 above).—As regards Bunni, some earlier scholars have put forth the view which others have rejected,

that under this name is to be understood the Nicodemus of
St John's Gospel [1]. We can find no better explanation. In
the treatise *Ta'anith* 20 a there is accordingly a certain Nicodemus (Nakdimon) ben Goryon mentioned, at whose prayer God
sent first rain, and then sunshine. At the close of the narrative
it is said : "It has been taught us, that his name was properly
Bunni : he was only called Nicodemus for this reason, because on
his account the sun shone out brightly (*nak'dah chammah*)." If
the Jews knew anything of Nicodemus the disciple of Jesus (and
how should they not, since it certainly made a great sensation
that a leader of the Pharisees had become a disciple of Christ, and
afterwards also frequently confessed himself to be such !) he was
then given the name Bunni, in order to distinguish him from the
Nicodemus of the Talmud, whose name through the abovementioned incident had become to a certain extent that of a saint.
As he on account of the miracle had lost his name Bunni, so the
Nicodemus of the New Testament, that he might not be confounded
with the other Nicodemus, received the name, which the latter
had had originally.—The name *Netzer* is unquestionably formed
from Notzri = Nazarene [2].—Nakkai admits of several conjectures.
By it Nicodemus may be meant again ; but it reminds us also of
Nicolaus or Nicanor (Acts vi. 5) ; or lastly there is contained in
it an allusion to the Nicolaitans (Apoc. ii. 6, 15), a word which is
equivalent to Balaamites. But Balaam is to the Talmudists the
type of Jesus, who in several places is expressly called by this
name [3] (pp. 53 ff.).—Lastly, the name Todah reminds us either of
the Apostle Thaddæus or of the Theudas of Acts v. 36.

----

[1] See Thilo, *Codex Apocryphus Novi Testamenti*, Leipzig, 1832, p. 550,
Rem.

[2] בן נצר is the representative of Edom in *Ber. R.* 76, beside Alexander
(מקדון) for Greece, Cyrus (קרום) for Persia, and (perhaps) Gordianus
(קרדידוס) for Rome. *Jalk. Schim.* to Daniel, § 1064, ed. of Salonica, 1521,
has the readings קרירום, קירום, מוקדון, בן נצור. Bar Neṣer was perhaps
a name of the Arabian usurper Odenath (about A.D. 260). See Grätz,
Geschichte der Juden, IV. 489. *Die talmudischen Texte*. [G. D.]

[3] Cp. as to the Nicolaitans, Hengstenberg, *The History of Balaam and
his Prophecies*, Berlin, 1842, p. 22.

To what an extent the conception of the number five attached itself solely and entirely to this narrative, while utterly non-existent outside it, and consequently quite unhistorical, we are furnished with further proof by the information which the Talmud gives us as to a sixth disciple, namely Jacob of K'phar S'khanya, whose acquaintance we have already (p. 63) made. That this Jacob was not an immediate disciple of Jesus we have already seen (p. 64): he cannot have passed for such until the time when Jesus was taken for a contemporary of Akiba. Hamburger's remark[1], "Jacob gave himself out as a disciple of Jesus" is uncommonly *naïf*. For according to his notion the Jews accepted from Jacob the statement that he was a disciple of Jesus, while they nevertheless knew still more certainly than ourselves that he was no such thing, seeing that they were not unaware that Jacob had never set eyes on Christ any more than themselves.

The questions how Jacob reached the honour of being called a disciple of Jesus and in general why he was kept in memory, are in fact the same. It was his thaumaturgic power, which led him to be placed in immediate relation with Jesus, the master of sorcery, and which in his time caused so great a sensation as never afterwards to be forgotten. The Talmud in several passages informs us of this power of working miracles.

In the Palestinian Talmud, *Shabbath* XIV. fol. 14 d at the bottom, we read: "It happened that R. Eleazar ben Dama[2] was bitten by a serpent. Then came Jacob of K'phar Sama, to heal him in the name of Jesus Pandēra. [In the Palestinian *Aboda Zara* fol. 40 d at the bottom[3], where the same narrative is found, the words are Jesus ben Pandēra.] But R. Ishmael suffered him not. Eleazar said to him : I will bring thee a proof, that he has a right to heal me. But he had no more time to utter the proof: for he died. R. Ishmael said to him : Blessed art thou, ben

---

[1] *Real-Encycl. für Bibel und Thalmud*, II. Art. *Eliezer*.

[2] Perhaps a nephew of the Ishmael who was an associate of Akiba. [A. W. S.]

[3] See p. 16*, xvii (a).

Dama, that thou wentest in peace from this world, and didst not break through the fence of the wise, because it is written (Eccles. x. 8): 'And whoso breaketh through a fence, a serpent shall bite him,' not, a serpent *has* bitten him, but (it means that) a serpent should not bite him in the time to come."

In the Bab. Talmud, *Aboda Zara*, 27 b, this history is worded thus : "It happened that ben Dama, son of R. Ishmael's sister, was bitten by a serpent. Then came Jacob of K'phar S'khanya to heal him. But R. Ishmael suffered him not. Ben Dama said : R. Ishmael, my brother, allow me to be healed by him, and I will bring thee a verse from the Torah, shewing that it is allowed. But he had not time to complete what he was saying : for his spirit departed from him and he died. Then R. Ishmael exclaimed over him : Happy art thou, ben Dama, that thy body is pure and that thy spirit has passed away in purity and that thou hast not transgressed the words of thy companions."

We find here the abovementioned Jacob engaged in the same work as before on the occasion of his meeting with R. Eliezer, namely, in the effort to win the Jews for Christ. And while on that occasion he made his attempt in the region of exposition, so here by the demonstration of his power over nature. But both times his aim was wrecked upon the fanaticism of the Jews. For however quiet the wording "he suffered him not," we have little right to think of a quiet scene, if we picture to ourselves the hatred and wrath, bordering on frenzy, which has from time to time seized the Jews on the approach of Christianity[1]. The horror which R. Ishmael had even of a miraculous cure, if it was effected in the name of Jesus, is betrayed by his stern resolve that his nephew should die rather than permit himself to be cured through the name of Jesus, as well as by his words spoken in truth from the depth of his heart : "Happy art thou, ben Dama, that thou hast passed away in purity." Ben Dama would have seemed to him defiled for ever, if he had been cured through the name of Jesus, and certainly, if, induced by the cure, he had bestowed on this Jesus his heart.

[1] See Appendix II.

Our history so confirms the power of the disciples, witnessed by the New Testament, to heal in the name of Jesus, that we must say : Here is a convincing proof of the truth of the miracles of Jesus and His disciples as recorded in the New Testament. Truly the name of Jesus is not an empty word, but a heavenly power, whose existence His enemies themselves cannot wholly get rid of by denial.

III. JESUS' END.

A. JESUS' CONDEMNATION.—In *Sanhedrin* 67 a[1] we read in the Mishnah : " In the case of all the transgressors indicated in the Torah as deserving of death no witnesses are placed in concealment except in case of the sin of leading astray to idolatry. If the enticer has made his enticing speech to two, these are witnesses against him, and lead him from the court of justice, and he is stoned.   But if he have used the expression not before two, but before one, *he* shall say to him : ' I have friends, who have a liking for that.'   But if he is cunning, and wishes to say nothing before the others, witnesses are placed in concealment behind the wall, and he says himself to the seducer : ' Now tell me once again, what thou wast saying to me, for we are alone.'   If he now repeats it, the other says to him : ' How should we forsake our heavenly Father, and go and worship wood and stone ? '   If then the enticer is converted, well and good ; but if he replies : ' This is our duty ; it is for our good,' then those who are standing behind the wall bring him before the court of justice, and he is stoned.—The Gemara both in the Babylonian and in the Palestinian Talmud (*Sanhedrin* VII. fol. 25 d, upper part[2]) adds the following (we quote in accordance with the last-named source) : ' The enticer is the idiot etc.—Lo, is he a wise man ?   No ; as an

---

[1] See p. 5*, i (b), of which however the first part of the above is a somewhat free rendering.   See it as given more literally in the " Translations." [A. W. S.]

[2] See p. 17*, xviii (b).

enticer, he is not a wise man ; as he is enticed, he is not a wise man.   How do they treat him so as to come upon him by surprise?   Thus; for the enticer two witnesses are placed in concealment in the innermost part of the house ; but he is made himself to remain in the exterior part of the house, wherein a lamp is lighted over him, in order that the witnesses may see him and distinguish his voice. Thus, for instance, they managed with the Son of Sot'da at Lud.   Against him two disciples of learned men were placed in concealment and he was brought before the court of justice, and stoned."   In the Babylonian Talmud the wording of the closing sentence is: " He was hung on the Sabbath of the Passover festival."—Again, a third passage in the Talmud (the Palestinian *Jebamoth*, XVI. 15 d in the lower part) speaks of the same thing in almost verbal agreement with the foregoing, on which account it is unnecessary to furnish the translation.

These three passages then, considered by themselves, bear the impress of being historical ; however strange one must find the law upon internal grounds. And Renan in his *Life of Jesus* (chap. 24) believes that he is bound to supplement by these Talmudic notices the New Testament account of the Trial of Jesus. But if the Talmud has romanced anywhere, it has done so here. Our task is to ascertain the points in the proceedings against Jesus, which formed the grain of seed for this Talmudic exuberance of growth.

But the first business is to set forth the absolute impossibility of the proceeding so distinctly pictured by the Talmud.   According to the Jewish law, as it is well known, no one could be tried and condemned without witnesses.   In the case of seduction to idolatry, the Mishnah accordingly says, and the Gemara repeats it, that the court obtains for itself the testimony of witnesses in the abovementioned crafty manner.   This presupposes that the seducer has never uttered his seducing words, publicly, not even once before two persons, but privately only to one individual, as well as that this one, far from being accessible to the seduction, has rather been determined forthwith to hand over the seducer to death on account of his expression.   Such a case is possible in itself. But neither according to the New Testament, nor (to which we here attach more weight) according to the universal conception of the Talmud, does this tally with the case of Jesus. According to the Talmud, He had seduced and led astray many of Israel, and this together with His sorcery formed the ground of His being condemned to death. Cp. *Sanhedrin* 43 a (see p. 85). If the actions and words of any man were public, such certainly according to the testimony of the Talmud were those of Jesus. That He had only wished to seduce one, and that this one would not be seduced, but handed Him over in a crafty way to the court of justice, is directly opposed to what we read in the New Testament, and in the Talmud as well. And now the Talmud does not merely assert this in the passages under discussion, but it also adduces the legal provision relating to it, in accordance with which Jesus was thus treated, and for the application of that provision it brings forward no other example but this unhistorical and impossible one.

Though the untying of this knot appears at the first view difficult, yet it is simple, if it can be demonstrated, (1) that the reverse of the Talmud's apparent assertion is the case ; in other words, that the Law, which is here said to have been brought into use against Jesus, owes its origin to nothing earlier than the narrative which deals with Jesus, and (2) that that narrative, from which the Law took its rise, while far from opposing the universal tradition, yet certainly at the same time not confirming it, and therefore defenceless in the presence of Rabbinic caprices, was much more simply framed, and first received its air of romance through the Law.

The emphasis is unmistakable, with which at the end of the Law the example of Jesus is adduced, especially in the Palestinian Talmud. For there the introductory particle "for so", or "that is to say, so" (shekken) points to this that there is no more pertinent example of the application of the Law, at all events that there are special grounds for adducing just that example as a voucher. Further, the agreement of both Talmuds is extremely significant. All this indisputably shews, that between Law and

S. 6

example there prevails something closer than a merely adventitious bond; that in the tradition which was transmitted until the Talmud was fixed by writing, from time to time the two were connected with each other in such a way that the Law was never thought or spoken of without this historical voucher belonging to it. Consequently the originator of the Law will already have the example subjoined. But then the example had a larger share in this combination with the Law than merely this, that it *was* an example; it can be shewn to have been actually the source of the Law. That Jesus's condemnation and execution, in which the Jewish people had taken their share with the most. excessive zeal, had not sunk into oblivion, is obvious. And in the same way we may assume, that the tradition referring to it was at some time tested by its relation to the Law. Now this tradition contained more than one particular, which was unique of its kind, or which must have appeared quite incredible. Since however it was held to be established that the proceedings against Jesus were legal, so it came to this, that the Law was inferred from the traditional history. That the matter stands thus is declared by the circumstance, that this history, as it is now to be understood from the Law, is opposed not merely in a point of detail, but in the main gist, to the otherwise universal tradition.

Our task is in the next place to distinguish the old historical outlines of the tradition, on which the Law was built up.—Of such outlines we believe that we can distinguish three. 1. Jesus was betrayed. The fact of the betrayal could not have easily sunk into oblivion, since the foes of Jesus must have used rather prolonged endeavours to bring Him into their power without causing excitement and disturbance. The details indeed had already sunk into oblivion; therefore it was made out that the betrayal takes place, because the disciple (Judas) was unwilling to allow himself to be seduced by Jesus (who forsooth passes for the seducer). 2. The remembrance of the fact that Jesus was betrayed in the night appears to have maintained itself in the lamp which betokens the night-time. 3. The duality of the witnesses; cp. Matt. xxvi. 20 and Deut. xvii. 6,

It is not difficult to combine these three particulars (Jesus shone upon by the night lamp, the traitor simulating friendship, the two witnesses who come forward) in such a way as to retain the tradition, which we recognise in the Palestinian Talmud. From the Mishnah it is much more difficult to recognise this tradition, since, as we have already seen, in shaping the law it dealt freely with the tradition. It has in the first place devised the case of not merely one, as in the traditional example, but two or more having been seduced by the seducer, and it has then held the witnesses lurking in concealment to be superfluous. But if the seducer only sought to seduce one, the treatment presented to us in the Jesus-tradition passes as a guiding case. Only the juristic subtlety characteristic of the Rabbis again dissected this case in such a way that it was at once set down as possible that the one seduced person might procure himself witnesses. Not until the seducer had avoided this trap, did there come to be applied the procedure which the Jesus-tradition contains. The Rabbinic colouring is here unmistakable; but not without reason are the words "to worship wood and stone" chosen. The seducing to idolatry has thereby preserved an expression which is strikingly in harmony with Jesus' worship of a stone appearing in the story of Jesus and Joshua ben P'rachya (see p. 41), so that we can scarcely avoid taking this feature in the Law we are reviewing as borrowed from the story of Jesus just named. If this assumption be correct, we might venture to conclude, that the Mishnic Law did not come into existence before the time of Eliezer or Aḳiba.

After the overthrow of Jerusalem the town of Lud, on account of the scholars who worked in it, acquired, especially at the beginning of the second century A.D., great importance[1], so that it was even called the second Jerusalem (Hamburger, *Real-Encyclopädie*, I. 722). In this town, according to the passage we are considering, Jesus was executed. We have already shewn (p. 38) how this statement was occasioned through the name of Aḳiba, inasmuch as the attacks upon the person of

[1] See note, p. 62. [A. W. S.]

Jesus by the scholar working in Lud imprinted themselves upon the memory to such an extent that the notion arose that Akiba and Jesus were contemporaries. In the face of this confusion of periods so distinct we cannot be surprised, that our passage also speaks of a Sanhedrin at Lud, whereas on the contrary a Sanhedrin has never had its seat there. After the overthrow of Jerusalem there was no longer any Sanhedrin at all. Soon indeed the Jewish people created for itself a new centre in the so-called Beth Din (literally, court-house) of Jabne[1]. But this was something essentially different from the old Sanhedrin; it lacked political privileges, and above all its legal decisions regarding religion had only a theoretic significance. And although it soon attained again to great power by exercising over the Jewish people an active jurisdiction, partly conceded, partly usurped, nevertheless Rabbinic Judaism has always had a distinct consciousness of the fact that the old Sanhedrin had ceased to exist; cp. Mishnah of *Sota*, ix. 11: which tells us that from the time that the Sanhedrin became extinct, all singing ceased at festive entertainments[2]. That in our passage (as also elsewhere occasionally) a Sanhedrin at Lud is mentioned, constitutes the less difficulty, as it was a very old tradition, that the execution of Jesus was carried out by the supreme council, which was only in name untrue, but in fact was quite correct.

Even though we were to bear in mind the Oriental imagination, still so hasty and bold, yet it is in any case impossible, that as early as immediately after the death of Akiba the notion grew up that Jesus had lived in Lud alongside of Akiba and his colleagues and had stood before a Sanhedrin in that city; but, as the shrinking of the tradition also proves, a considerable time must have elapsed thereafter. We may not indeed extend too much the time between the death of Akiba and the rise of the notion that Jesus had lived in Lud, etc., since the Mishnah, to which the law here discussed belongs, received its final shape as early as the year 220 A.D.[3] at the hands of R. Jehudah the Prince.

---

[1] See Neubauer *Géog. du Th.* pp. 73 ff.

[2] Schürer, *History of the Jewish People*, Div. ii. vol. i. pp. 173, note.

[3] Or somewhat earlier [A. W. S.].

B. JESUS' EXECUTION.—While the execution of Jesus was only briefly and incidentally mentioned in *Sanhedrin* 67 a, the extract, which we now desire to consider, speaks expressly of this execution and the preparations for it.

Sanhedrin 43 a[1] runs thus : " But there is a tradition ; On the Sabbath of the Passover festival Jesus was hung. But the herald went forth before him for the space of forty days, while he cried : ' Jesus goeth forth to be executed, because he has practised sorcery and seduced Israel and estranged them from God. Let any one who can bring forward any justifying plea for him, come and give information concerning it.' But no justifying plea was found for him, and so he was hung on the Sabbath of the Passover festival. Ulla has said : ' But dost thou think that he belongs to those for whom a justifying plea is sought? He was a very seducer, and the Allmerciful has said (Deut. xiii. 8): 'Thou shalt not spare him, nor conceal him.' However in Jesus' case it was somewhat different, for his place was near those in power."

This narrative in its purport fits in precisely with *Sanhedrin* 67 a. We are already aware how little the Talmudic reports about Jesus cohere or even harmonize. So much the more does it strike us, that *Sanhedrin* 43 a quite plainly forms the continuation of *Sanhedrin* 67 a, and the assumption forces itself upon us that originally the two pieces were one. But if this be the case, then the omission of the word "Lud" in the extract now to be discussed is to be explained by its being quite unnecessary, after it had been expressed shortly before, and the omission of this word is not a token that our extract belongs to a somewhat older time than the former, namely, to a time in which the notion that Jesus and Akiba had lived in Lud as contemporaries, did not yet exist.

That the two extracts, originally cohering, underwent a severance on the occasion of the Rabbinical discussion, was natural. We saw that the tradition contained in the former extract was viewed with the aim of obtaining a clear juristic

[1] See p. 15*, xv.

knowledge of the proceedings against Jesus on their legal side. The law, which was deduced from the case, is laid down in the Mishnah. In that part of the tradition which is contained in *Sanhedrin* 43 a we have a difficulty of another kind to deal with. The procedure which was observed with respect to a condemned person was the following. While the criminal was conducted to the place of execution, there stood at the door of the court an usher, whose duty was to give a signal by the waving of a flag, if through any fresh pieces of evidence a reconsideration of the case were called for and the condemned person should have to be brought back. Another messenger of the court was posted on horseback further on the road, in order to pass on quickly the signal which might be given with the flag, and to fetch the condemned person back. A herald moved in advance of the condemned and cried : "So and so in accordance with the testimony of such and such witnesses, on account of such and such a crime, at such and such a place, at such and such a time, has been condemned to death ; whoso has anything to adduce in his defence, let him come and say it." In case that a new ground of defence was adduced, the condemned was brought back to the court, that they might test its validity and, if need be, alter the sentence. But if no disclosure of fresh evidence followed upon the way to the place of execution the sentence was carried into effect (Hamburger, ii. p. 1152).—Our extract then informs us, in contrast to these provisions, that between the sentence and execution of Jesus forty days were permitted to elapse. Ulla, a Palestinian scholar of the beginning of the 4th century, who, after first emigrating to Babylonia, repeatedly returned to Palestine to visit his old home, from the employment of the old Boraitha as evidence for the usual course of justice in early time, took occasion to put to the unconscious Babylonians the question : Is Jesus then to be considered as having belonged to those for whom a justifying plea was actually sought, on account of which He might have been delivered from the death-penalty, He who had deserved death ten times over? "Of course," answered Ulla himself, "this was not the question ; but, inasmuch as Jesus was related to the authorities, not only had the accustomed law to be observed, but by way of exception the period of respite had to be extended to forty days, that the Romans might not afterwards be able to declare the capital sentence to be unjust and annoy the Jews."—How then did Ulla come to assert that Jesus was related to the (Roman) authorities? It can scarcely be taken as the product of simple imagination. A grain of historical truth must lie at the bottom of it. What is this? Now we are of opinion that the reluctance of Pontius Pilate to allow Jesus to be executed was a particular in the history of the Passion, which, for the Jews, could not so quickly sink into oblivion. While the doctors of the Law panted for the blood of Jesus, the Roman governor, overcome by His sublimity and purity, could only with difficulty bring himself to confirm the capital sentence. The saying, that Jesus was related to the Roman authorities, forms a *precipitate* from the recollection of this line of conduct.—How right we are in seeing Pontius Pilate behind the Roman government, is proved by the fact that to the latest time this name has remained in the memory of the Jews, and indeed in connexion with the person of Jesus[1]: the Targum Sheni on the Book of Esther (iii. 1) names Pilate also with Jesus among the ancestors of Haman (cp. also p. 60).

On the other hand the forty days rest upon no kind of tradition in the history of Jesus. For where in the history of the Passion is there to be found a sentence of significance with the number forty? It may be that we are to call to mind the forty days' fast before Easter, observed perhaps at quite an early period, at least here and there, in the Christian Church, and later universally. The Christians—so the Jews may have thought— fast forty days in remembrance of the Passion of Christ, which thus continued for forty days[2].

---

[1] The Jews also of Mahommed's time *boasted* of having put Jesus to death. *Sura*, iv. 156.

[2] If anything at all of fact lies at the bottom of the number forty in *Sanhedrin* 43 a, it might perhaps rather be permitted to think of the Saviour's forty days' fast of Matt. iv. 2. According to Synagogue theology

Yet a few words on the clause "and they hanged him on the Sabbath of the Passover festival." The date, as we see, has impressed itself sharply on the memory of the Jews ; it was also in itself a noteworthy date, this date of the execution of a memorable man.   Accordingly we shall not venture to doubt that the manner of execution also was fully noted.   The expression indeed " they hanged him," seems doubtless on a superficial observation surprising.   But for the Jews of the time of Jesus, who in contrast to the Rabbinism of to-day did not cast the responsibility for the death of Jesus upon the Romans, but, as was equitable, claimed this deed for themselves, it was natural to make use of the word *talah* (תלה), *to hang*, familiar to them on account of Deut. xxi. 22, 23.   Even the Apostle Paul, referring to this passage of the Law, has written (Gal. iii. 13) " Christ redeemed us from the curse of the law, having become a curse for us ; for it is written, Cursed is every one that hangeth on a tree."   Further for the elucidation of the whole matter we may here adduce the following from G. Dalman's learned and profound study " Der Gottesname Adonaj und seine Geschichte " (Berlin, 1889, H. Reuther), p. 46 f.: "Josephus says (*Ant.* iv. 8. 6): 'Let him that has blasphemed God be stoned and hung up for a whole day, and be buried in dishonour and darkness.' Stoning, hanging, and a dishonoured burial are thus the legal punishment of the blasphemer.   The hanging is here only intended as the ignominious exposure of the corpse of the person executed.   The stoning of the blasphemer is gathered too from Lev. xxiv. 16, and thereby proof is furnished that this passage was authoritatively taken not of the mere utterance of the Divine Name, but of its use in blasphemy.   It was on the ground of this piece of the Law that Jesus was condemned to death as a blasphemer, according to Matt.

---

fasting belongs to the methods of atonement. Cp. Weber, *System*, p. 305. The forty days' fast of Jesus may have given occasion to the view that the execution of the capital sentence was postponed for forty days. It might also be possible to think of the forty days between the Resurrection and the Ascension. [H. L. S.]

xxvi. 65, 66 ; and Mark xiv. 63, 64 ; cp. John xix. 7"[1]. When Joel, in his "Blicke in die Religions-geschichte zu Anfang des zweiten christlichen Jahrhunderts" II. (1883), pp. 48 ff., desires to prove that the Jews can have had nothing to do with the Cruci-fixion of Jesus, he means of course that Jesus had not spoken an actual blasphemy. But, as N. Brüll[2] rightly remarks, according to Rabbinic law, everyone, "who stretches out his hand against one ʿikkar, one fundamental article in the Law,' was to be looked upon as a blasphemer and to be punished." See Siphre[3] on Deut. xxi. 22. On this principle Jesus' prophetic utterance before the court of justice (Mark xiv. 62) in which He adjudged to Himself a share in the Divine honour, might be designated as blasphemy and be made the ground of His condemnation. If the people, advised by the members of the tribunal (Matt. xxvii. 22 ; Mark xv. 13, 14[4] ; John xix. 6) desired of Pilate crucifixion (hanging) as the mode of death, this, we may feel sure, had not for its reason that in Deut. (xxi. 22, 23) for every executed person a supplementary hanging is enjoined, but because, as in fact ap-pears from that passage of Josephus, hanging already at that time belonged to the special punishment of the blasphemer. Since stoning did not figure in Roman criminal law, hanging at least, which in the view of the Romans was applicable as the punishment of the insurgent, had to be carried out in the case of Jesus. The tzʾlibeh or tzʾlib jatheh, with which doubtless the cru-cifixion of Jesus was demanded of Pilate, contains the word cog-nate to that in Onk.'s Targum of Deut. xxi. 22, 23, for the hang-ing of the blasphemer of God. The cause of the application of hanging to the blasphemer is to be sought in the words of Deut. xxi. 23, " For he that is hanged is a curse of God." The LXX. indeed rendered, " Everyone who hangeth on a tree is accursed by God." The Rabbis however understood kilʾlath ʾlohim of the cursing of God, which is to be punished with hanging.

---

[1] Add Luke xxii. 70, 71. [A. W. S.]

[2] *Jahrbücher für jüd. Gesch. u. Lit.* VII. p. 96.

[3] A Rabbinic commentary on Numb. and Deut. [A. W. S.]

[4] Add Luke xxiii. 21, 23. [A. W. S.]

As an *addendum* to this we mention a passage out of the
Targum Sheni to the Book of Esther vii. 9[1]. After having related that Haman appealed to Mordecai for mercy tearfully, but
in vain, it says: "And when Haman saw that his words were
not heard, he began a lamentation and weeping for himself in
the midst of the garden of the palace." And then there is
added: "He answered and spake thus: Hear me, ye trees and
all ye plants, which I have planted since the days of the creation.
The son of Hammedatha is about to ascend to the lecture-room of
Ben Pandēra." And then one tree after another excuses itself
for not allowing Haman to be hung upon it, till at last the
cedar proposes that Haman be hung upon the gallows appointed
by him for Mordecai and already set up. Consequently by
'ascending to the lecture-room of Ben Pandēra' is to be understood in general being hung on the tree of ignominy. For
plainly that is the matter in hand. Jesus is to the Jews simply
the "hanged" (*talui*, now commonly pronounced *tôle*), and
accordingly the gallows is reckoned as the equipment peculiarly
adapted to Him. But so far as Jesus was the Founder of a new
doctrine, it was an obvious jeer, to call the gallows the "lecture-
room of Ben Pandēra." This jeer acquires a specially venomous
flavour through its being God, in Whose mouth the words are
placed, the Holy God, Whose Son Jesus had declared Himself to
be, and as Whose Son He was held in honour by the Christians.
Certainly the surface look of the arrangement of the sentences
creates the appearance[2] of Haman's being the speaker; but the
connexion marks this conception as impossible. For how is it to
be supposed that Haman, in his anxiety about his life, asks of
the trees in order permission to be hanged on them? How is it
possible that Haman should speak of trees and plants which he
had planted since the creation? We may add that during the
conversation one of the trees, the date palm, addresses God

---

[1] See p. 17* xx.

[2] Paulus Cassel, for example, has allowed himself to be deceived by this
appearance. See *Das Buch Esther*, i. (Berlin, 1878), p. 296, and *Aus Literatur
und Geschichte* (Leipzig and Berlin, 1885), App. p. 66. [H. L. S.]

direct. Perhaps the negligence in expression first arose through an error having crept into the text. The rare form *aksandria* (אכסנדריא) is certainly not, with Levy[1], to be corrected to *Alexandria*, but must be explained by ἔξεδρα[2], if we are not actually to adopt that reading.

C. *The rending of the veil.* On this subject we will listen to von Hofman's words[3]: "As the heavens again became clear, after the sufferings of Jesus were ended; as the veil, which had interposed between the heavens and the earth, was rent at His departure; so also the veil of the temple was rent, which separated the Holy of Holies from the Holy place; and truly this was not accomplished without eye-witnesses. For Jesus died at the hour at which the priest in the sanctuary was occupied in presenting the incense-offering, and in lighting the sacred lamps. In the Gemara[4] is the tradition that once, forty years before the destruction of the temple, its folding gates burst open of themselves. This appears to be a weaker version of the incident related by the evangelists. For the date forty years before the destruction of the temple coincides with the year of Rome 783, in which year according to our reckoning the death of the Lord took place. It is however conceivable that the Jews, instead of a rending of the veil, which cut off the Holy of Holies, preferred to speak of an opening of the temple gates. For they must have understood full well, that the first was an adverse sentence passed upon the permanence of their worship, as a thing which rested altogether upon the severance between the Holy place and the Holy of Holies."

---

[1] *Wörterb. über den Targumim*, I. 31.

[2] So rightly explained, *e.g.* by Lebrecht in *Hammazkir*, IX. (1869), p. 146; P. Cassel, *Aus Lit. u. Gesch.*, App. p. 66.—The Greek word, *Exedra, a hall*, occurs already in the Mishnah (*Ohaloth*, XI. 2). [H. L. S.]

[3] *Die bibl. Geschichte Neuen Testaments*, Nordlichen, 1883, p. 259.

[4] *Joma*, 39 b, ת"ר ארבעים שנה קודם חורבן הבית לא היה גורל עולה בימין...והיו דלתות ההיכל נפתחות מאליהן.

The Pal. Talmud, *Joma*, VI. 43 c fin., gives the words of Jochanan as follows: לָמָה אַתָּה מְבַהֲלֵנוּ (cur terres *nos*?). [H. L. S.]

This way of taking the Gemara passage seems to me to be less probable than the following explanation :

It is a fact that the doors of the temple burst open on the occasion of the Death of Jesus, and that, immediately after or contemporaneously with the rending of the veil. With the fact that the Holy of Holies was at an end, the Holy place also existed no more. And as the former was indicated by a sign, so no less was the latter ; only that the Evangelists, as always, so also here, recorded only the most essential (the rending of the veil). Hofman has rightly seen, why the Gemara has been completely silent as to the most essential, while on the other hand it has recorded that which was less essential, and which moreover was seen by the laity. We have thus here presented to us a very probable completion of the Gospel account, for which we must thank the Talmud.

D. JESUS IN THE UNSEEN WORLD. *Gittin* 57 a[1]: "Onkelos bar Kalonikos, nephew of Titus, desired to secede to Judaism. He conjured up the spirit of Titus and asked him : Who is esteemed in that world ? He answered : The Israelites. Onkelos asked further : Ought one to join himself to them ? He answered : Their precepts are too many; thou canst not keep them; go rather hence and make war upon them in this world; so shalt thou become a head; for it is said (Lam. i. 5): 'Their adversaries are become the head,' i.e. Every one, that vexeth the Israelites, becomes a head. Onkelos asked the spirit: Wherewith art thou judged ? He answered : With that, which I have appointed for myself : each day my ashes are collected and I am judged ; then I am burnt and the ashes scattered over the seven seas.—Thereupon Onkelos went and conjured up the spirit of Balaam. He asked him : Who is esteemed in that world ? The spirit answered : The Israelites. Onkelos asked further : Ought one to join himself to them ? The spirit said : Seek not their peace and their good alway. Onkelos asked : Wherewith art thou judged ? The spirit answered : With boiling pollution[2].— Thereupon Onkelos went and conjured up the spirit of Jesus.

---

[1] See p. 17*, xxi. (a).   [2] Samenerguss.

He asked Him: Who is esteemed in that world? The spirit
answered: The Israelites. Onkelos asked further: Ought one
to join himself to them? The spirit said: Seek their good and
not their ill. He who toucheth them, toucheth the apple of His
eye. Onkelos asked: Wherewith art thou judged? The spirit
said: With boiling filth[1]. For the Teacher[2] has said: He who
scorneth the words of the wise, is judged with boiling filth.—See
what a distinction there is between the apostates of Israel and
the heathen prophets!"

The unhistorical character of this narrative follows from its
contents. Not that we are to be considered as belonging to
those, to whom a conjuring up of the dead appears impossible, or
as finding it ridiculous that a heathen, who, after he had studied
the doctrines of the Jews, has determined to become a proselyte,
still desires first to question the dead concerning his step. The
reality of the one is sufficiently witnessed by the Scriptures, and
the possibility of the other must be granted in the case of a man,
who even with every inclination to Judaism is nevertheless still
a heathen and has not yet thrown off the works of heathenism.
Also it is thoroughly natural that Onkelos should summon the
spirits of such as passed with him for enemies of Judaism, and
that he exercises a well-considered choice, in that he calls up
from Hades first two heathen, of whom the one (Titus) had
earned a lasting evil memory through the overthrow of Jerusalem, and the other (Balaam) through his attempt to destroy
Israel by means of impure idolatry[3]; then an Israelite (Jesus),
who as an opponent of the Jewish teachers had not His like.

But by a string of other features the whole narrative is
shewn to be a product of Jewish national poetry. If the Spirit
of lies had once begun by means of his lying spirits to extol the
lot of the Israelites in the other world to him who contemplated
seceding to Judaism, he would surely have been obliged con-

[1] Kot.

[2] *Daamar mar.* The same formula of citation occurs, p. 41.

[3] From this crime of Balaam the punishment also here imposed on him
is explained.

sistently to recommend to Onkelos that secession. This however does not take place, but the two heathen advise making war upon Israel, while only the Israelite Jesus advises friendship with Israel. This is a thoroughly Jewish idea. For the Jew is too proud to recognise foreign testimony : he knows no more weighty authority than the Jew. Onkelos did not venture on the advice of a heathen to secede to Judaism, but only on the advice of a Jew, whose judgment in this case weighed the heavier, as He (naturally, according to the view of the Jews) had been in no way a friend of Judaism, and now found Himself undergoing the severest punishment, the full justice of which He acknowledges.—Also the distinction of the punishments of the unseen world allows us clearly to recognise the origin of the history on the soil of Jewish poetry. One national feature has here dislodged the other. Jewish opinion in the abstract would have been, that the Israelite would have to undergo a much slighter penalty than the two heathen. Instead of this, the penal tortures of Jesus exceed those of the two non-Israelites. For yet stronger than the consciousness of having in Jesus a fellow-countryman was ever and anon the hatred towards Him, of which it must be said that it has become the most national feature of Judaism since the rejection of Christ, as then it has also found in our narrative the grossest conceivable expression.

Since the narrative, as we saw, is fictitious, we assume, on account of the importance which the person of Jesus has in it, that the leading thought of the fiction culminates in fact in that person : the extolled secession of the illustrious Onkelos to Judaism has to be commended by Jesus in such a manner, that He has not only out of the deepest punishment put forth His exhortation, but also has depicted and recognised as justified this His punishment which yet has absolutely no reference to Onkelos's design.

The punishment of "boiling filth" is perhaps a thing first invented with regard to Jesus, and an expression of hate towards the most hated of all hated men ; for in the exceptional position which Jesus assumes in every respect, it is easily to be supposed that Judaism, which was very ingenious in new conceptions with regard to the state of things in the unseen world[1], in the case of Jesus did not content itself with a penalty already assigned to others. In fact we find the "boiling filth" elsewhere only in one place, namely *Erubin*, 21 b, where with reference to the Divine character of the words of the doctors of the Law it is said in the name of Rab Acha bar Ulla ; "from this [from Eccles. xii. 12] it follows, that he who jeers at the words of the doctors of the Law, is punished by boiling filth." If in this passage the words "like Jesus of Nazareth" have not been struck out by the *Censure*[2] or otherwise fallen away from the text, they may nevertheless be added in thought. That by "boiling filth" we are not to understand a division in hell, is clearly deduced from the parallelism : it is said of Balaam, that he was punished with boiling pollution. Conditions are meant, methods of punishment. It was not till post-Talmudic times, that evidently through the desire to develop and colour all the monstrous statements of the Talmud about Jesus (cp. the *Tol'doth Jeshu*), the "boiling filth" was made into a division of hell, and the following teaching put forth : The "boiling filth" is the lowest abode in hell, into which there sinks every foulness of the souls, which sojourn in the upper portions. It is also as a secret chamber, and every superfluity, in which there is no spark of holiness, falls thereinto. For this reason it is called "boiling filth," according to the mysterious words of Is. xxviii. 8 : "There is so much vomit and filthiness, that there is no place clean," as it is said in Is. xxx. 52 : "Thou shalt call it filth[3]" (*'Emek hammelech* 135 c, chap. 19. See Eisenmenger, *Entdecktes Judenthum*, II. 335 ff.).

---

[1] So e. g. according to *Baba Bathra*, 74 a, the hell for the Korahites is each month fashioned anew, and they boil therein like meat in the pot.

[2] The Talmudic Commentary Tosaphoth on *Erubin* [see p. 18*, xxi. (*b*)], which was not subjected to the *Censure*, refer to *Gittin*, 57. But the connexion with Eccles. xii. 12 seems to indicate that this penalty was not invented for Jesus. [H. L. S.]

[3] According to this (erroneous) interpretation, צָאָה=צֵאָה of Deut. xxviii. 14, Ezek. iv. 12. [A. W. S.]

Such gross ideas are wont to arise at a time of great excitement. Hamburger[1] remarks: " The phantastic ideas as to the punishments of hell arose in the times of the terrible persecutions directed against Israel, where the Jews had to find comfort and relief in dealing with the further world, the abode of righteousness." So Wünsche[2]: " In order to strengthen the confidence in a Divine retribution, the Rabbis laid on the colours strongly."— Onkelos belongs to the age of Akiba. From the political features of this time we may also comprehend the charge against Jesus which our passage contains : He had mocked at the words of the learned in Holy Writ : a charge (according to Jewish conception) very well founded, which was with much eagerness made prominent, inasmuch as the persecution of the Jews on the part of the Romans at the time of Akiba, had specially to do with the doctors of the Law, who formed the living pillars of Judaism. The old hatred against Jesus, which had so severely shaken all respect for Rabbinic reputation, blazed out with new violence, when the Romans likewise although in quite a different manner made war upon the authorities of Judaism.

CONCLUSION.

We are at the end of our investigation and elucidation of the passages in the Talmud which refer to Jesus, and now place before ourselves by way of summary its result.

Two points are continually presented to us in a striking way: 1st. The extraordinary paucity and scantiness of those accounts, 2nd. Their fabulous character.

Unattacked by Christianity, rather seeing their highest ideal in the actual persecution of that faith (cp. the *Acts of the Apostles*), thrown back upon their own oral tradition, which not only, like all oral tradition, was in danger of being dulled and distorted, and at last of completely disappearing from the memory, but also was strongly influenced by hatred towards Jesus,

---

[1] *Real-Encyclopädie*, I. 529.
[2] A. Wünsche, *Jahrbücher für protest. Theologie*, 1880, p. 511.

the Jews only retained some main features of His history in their memory, namely: of His ministry only the general account, that He was a seducer of the people and a sorcerer and a fool, who had given Himself out to be God; somewhat more of His Trial and Execution, since in the latter the Jewish people had taken part with such vast excitement. Accordingly later, especially in and since the time of R. Akiba, from this shrinking down of the history to a few points, there came to be a prevalent need for more stories of Jesus. Hence the origin of the impulse to develop and season with ridicule what they still possessed. Not troubling themselves about chronology, they found in an old anonymous narrative a story about Jesus (see pp. 41 ff.); from isolated fragments there was formed independently a uniform picture (cp. Jesus' condemnation and execution, pp. 79 ff.); at last they surrendered themselves to pure fiction, to give vent to their scorn (cp. the five disciples, pp. 71 ff.). Expressions of scorn, words of ridicule, piquant, and therefore received with applause, served as the basis of new fables (cp. the names Pandēra and Stada, pp. 7 ff., as well as the story in *Kallah* 18 b, pp. 33 ff.). How great had been the shrinkage as regards the recollections of Jesus, and how powerfully then the reconstruction of His history wrought upon the feelings of the Jewish people, is seen from the singular fact, that Akiba, the man who took the most active part in this fresh ill-treatment of Jesus, was plainly held in the most vivid recollection as regards his relation to Him and to Christianity, so much so that Jesus was actually taken for his contemporary.

Upon this time of rank growth of stories concerning Jesus there followed later again a time in which almost no intercourse with Christians took place. In it the stories of Jesus were more and more left on one side, and so of the many productions of the time, which we propose to call the Akiba-time, only that very small amount has been kept in mind, which is put before us in the Talmud. But that the hatred towards Jesus merely slumbered, and only waited a touch, in order to break forth again, is seen from the Mary-legend, pp. 27 ff.

From the history of the origin of the Talmudic stories about Jesus may be understood not only the lack of resemblance in these stories to the actual history of Jesus, but also the impossibility of obtaining a uniform picture from them. Moreover this has never yet been attempted by a Jew, but these "precious stones" have ever been considered and cherished only in their individual capacities. That they are not precious stones, but rubbish only, our investigation has sufficiently proved.

The perception of the slender value of the Talmudic notices of Jesus, necessarily directs the Jew to whom Jesus is surely an extraordinarily important Personage, to the reading of the New Testament.—But what we Christians have gained from the foregoing investigation is a weapon for the right hand and for the left. For each thoughtful Jew we have shewn the unfitness of the Talmud to be reckoned as a real source for the history of Jesus ; while we point the non-Jew, if he be an unbeliever, to the testimony of the Talmud that Jesus wrought "Egyptian," i.e. unwonted, miracles (pp. 45 ff.), as well as to its repeated reference to the miracles wrought by the disciples through His name (pp. 77 ff.).

Lastly, we may be thankful that the papal attempt to destroy the Talmudic passages concerning Jesus was doomed to fail.

APPENDIX I. (See p. 2.)

SINCE everyone has not the writings of Justin at hand, we venture to offer some important extracts from them bearing on this subject. We quote in accordance with the edition of J. C. Th. Otto, Jena, 1843:— "The Jews regard us as foes and opponents, and kill, and torture us, if they have the power. In the lately-ended Jewish war Bar Kokh'ba, the instigator of the Jewish revolt, caused Christians alone to be dragged to terrible tortures, whenever they would not deny and revile Jesus Christ[1]." "The Jews hate us, because we say that Christ is already come, and because we point out that He, as had been prophesied, was crucified by them[2]."—"Therefore we pray both for you Jews and for all other men who hate us, that you place yourselves in company with us, and against those, whom His works, and the miracles now still wrought through the invoking of His Name, and His teaching, as well as the prophecies concerning Him as wholly undefiled and blameless, all unite to admonish that they should vomit forth no revilings against Jesus Christ, but believe on Him[3]." "The high-priests of your nation and your teachers have caused that the name of Jesus should be profaned and reviled through the whole world[4]."—"Ye have killed the Just and His prophets before Him. And now ye despise those, who hope in Him and in God, the King over all and Creator of all things, who has sent Jesus; ye despise and dishonour them, as much as in you lies, in that in your synagogues ye curse those who believe in Christ. Ye only lack the power, on account of those who hold the reins of government, to treat us with violence. But as often as ye have had this power, ye have also done this[5]." "In your synagogues ye

---

[1] *Apology*, i. chap. 31.   [2] *Ibid.* chap. 36.
[3] *Dialogue with Trypho*, chap. 35.   [4] *Ibid.* chap. 117.
[5] *Ibid.* chap. 16.

curse all who have become Christians, and the same is done by the other nations, who give a practical turn to the curse, in that when any one merely acknowledges himself a Christian, they put him to death[1]." " Nay, ye have added thereto, that Christ taught those impious, unlawful, horrible actions, which ye disseminate as charges above all against those who acknowledge Christ as Teacher and as the Son of God[2]."— " Yet revile not the Son of God, and hearken not to the Pharisees as teachers, that after prayer ye should ill-treat the King of Israel with scoffs, as they have been taught you by the rulers of the synagogue[3]." —" As far as depends on you and the rest of mankind, each Christian is driven not only from his possession, but completely out of the world: ye permit no Christian to live[4]."—"Your hand is stretched out for ill-doing. For instead of experiencing repentance for having put Christ to death, ye hate us who through Him believe on God and the Father of all things, and ye put us to death as often as ye have the power, and ye continually curse Christ and His adherents, whereas we all pray for you as in general for all men" (after the wording of Matt. v. 44; Luke vi. 27 f.)[5],—"Your teachers exhort you to permit yourselves no conversation whatever with us[6]."—"There does not press upon other nations so heavy an offence against us and Christ as upon you, who are the originators of the preconceived evil opinion, which the nations cherish concerning Christ and us, His disciples. For since ye have attached Him the only blameless and righteous One to the Cross, ye have not only made no amends for your atrocious action, but at that time ye sent forth chosen men from Jerusalem, to proclaim throughout the world, that there is a new sect, namely, the Christians, arisen, which reverence no God, and to spread abroad what all who know us not maintain concerning us. It was your most earnest endeavour that bitter, dark, unjust charges should be put into circulation throughout the whole world against that sole spotless and righteous Light, which was sent from God to men[7]."—"The Jews make war against the Christians as against a foreign nation, and the Greeks (*i.e.* the Gentiles) persecute them; but their enemies can allege no ground of hostility[8]."

[1] *Dialogue with Trypho*, chap. 96.
[2] *Ibid.* chap. 108.
[3] *Ibid.* chap. 137.
[4] *Ibid.* chap. 110.
[5] *Ibid.* chap. 133.
[6] *Ibid.* chap. 112.
[7] *Ibid.* chap. 17.
[8] *Letter to Diognetus*, chap. 5.

APPENDIX II. (See p. 78.)

A RARE exception may be supplied by the following case, which is furnished us from the life of John Kasp. Schade, that pious Berlin pastor, often mentioned in the history of pietism along with Spener and Francke:—"What the power of God effected through him was also acknowledged by the Jews. About two years before his death (1698) a Jewish father accompanied by the Jewish schoolmaster came to him, and begged of him earnestly that he would pray over his son, who was possessed with an evil spirit, inasmuch as all Rabbinic prayers and ceremonies had availed nought. Schade declared himself willing to comply with this request, adding however as a condition, that he could not pray over the child otherwise than in the name of Jesus of Nazareth. Consent was given. Schade went to the Jew's residence, and by his prayer procured an improvement from that moment in the boy and deliverance from the complaint. From this time forward Schade was held in great consideration and respect by the Jews in Berlin; many of them visited him with frequency and held him to be a prophet. And when the Christian populace, out of rage against this preacher of repentance, desired on the day of his funeral to force open his grave, the Christians were put to shame by the Jews, inasmuch as the latter spoke with indignation of such an outrage to the grave of a pious man." (See "Christoterpe" by A. Knapp, 1853, pp. 151 f.; comp. also I. de le Roi, *Die evang. Christenheit und die Juden*, vol. I. p. 215.)

SUMMARY OF THE CONTENTS.

I. GENERAL INDEX.

Abbahu, 50
Aboda zara, 13, 32
Acha bar Ulla, 95
Ahab, 54
Ahithopel, 54 ff.
Akiba, 6, 14 f., 19, 25, 32 ff., 38 f.,
  45, 55 f., 62 ff., 74, 83 ff., 96 f.
Aksandria (Alexandria), 91
Aksanga (inn, hostess), 41
Alexander, 76
Alexander Jannæus, see Jannai.
Amoraim, 9
Angel of death, 27 ff.
Awen-gillajon, 13
'Awon-gillajon, 13, 70

Baba Bathra, 95
Bacchus, 24
Balaam, 14, 53 ff., 60 f., 92 f.
Bar Koch'ba, 6, 13 ff., 32, 74 f., 99
Bar Kōzēba, 13
Bar Neṣer, 76
Ben-Azzai, see Simeon Ben A.
Ben-Dama, 78
Ben-Sōt'da, 15, 80
Ben-Sṭada (Sṭara), see Sṭada.
Beth-din, 84
Beth-galja, 13
Beth-karja, 13
Beth-lehem, massacre of Innocents
  at, 14
Bethome, crucifixion of Jews at, 42
Bibi bar Abbai, 28 ff.

Bilga, priestly course of, 20
Boy with uncovered head, story of,
  34 ff.
Brickbat, worship of, 41
Brüll, *Jahrbücher u. s. w.*, 89
Bunni, 72 ff.

Caricature-names, 12
Cassel's *Aus Litteratur u. s. w.*, 12 f.,
  18, 90.
Celsus, 19, 22, 25
Censure, Jewish collections of pas-
  sages excised by the, 1. See also
  Talmud.
Chagigah, 33, 42
Chanina, 59 f.
Chelḳath M'choḳeḳ, 7
Chia, see Joseph bar C.
Chia bar Abba (= C. Rabbah), 50 f.
Coronel's *Commentarios etc.*, 35
Cyrus, 76

Dalman's *Der Gottesname u. s. w.*,
  88
de le Roi, *Die Evang. Christenheit
  u. s. w.*, 101
Delitzsch, *Ein Tag u. s. w.*, 34
Diospolis, see Lud.
Disciples, the five, 71 ff.
Doeg, 54 ff.

Egypt (Jesus in), 41 ff.; character of
  E. for magic, 48 f.

II. INDEX OF PASSAGES.

CAMBRIDGE : PRINTED BY C. J. CLAY, M.A. AND SONS, AT THE UNIVERSITY PRESS.

THE JEWISH PEOPLE

HISTORY • RELIGION • LITERATURE

AN ARNO PRESS COLLECTION

Agus, Jacob B. **The Evolution of Jewish Thought:** From Biblical Times to the Opening of the Modern Era. 1959

Ber of Bolechow. **The Memoirs of Ber of Bolechow (1723-1805).** Translated from the Original Hebrew MS. with an Introduction, Notes and a Map by M[ark] Vishnitzer. 1922

Berachya. **The Ethical Treatises of Berachya, Son of Rabbi Natronai Ha-Nakdan:** Being the Compendium and the Masref. Now edited for the First Time from MSS. at Parma and Munich with an English Translation, Introduction, Notes, etc. by Hermann Gollancz. 1902

Bloch, Joseph S. **My Reminiscences.** 1923

Bokser, Ben Zion, **Pharisaic Judaism in Transition:** R. Eliezer the Great and Jewish Reconstruction After the War with Rome. 1935

Dalman, Gustaf. **Jesus Christ in the Talmud, Midrash, Zohar, and the Liturgy of the Synagogue.** Together with an Introductory Essay by Heinrich Laible. Translated and Edited by A. W. Streane. 1893

Daube, David. **The New Testament and Rabbinic Judaism.** 1956

Davies, W. D. **Christian Origins and Judaism.** 1962

Engelman, Uriah Zevi. **The Rise of the Jew in the Western World:** A Social and Economic History of the Jewish People of Europe. Foreword by Niles Carpenter. 1944

Epstein, Louis M. **The Jewish Marriage Contract:** A Study in the Status of the Woman in Jewish Law. 1927

Facets of Medieval Judaism. 1973. New Introduction by Seymour Siegel

The Foundations of Jewish Life: Three Studies. 1973

Franck, Adolph. **The Kabbalah, or, The Religious Philosophy of the Hebrews.** Revised and Enlarged Translation [from the French] by Dr. I. Sossnitz. 1926

Goldman, Solomon. **The Jew and The Universe.** 1936

Gordon, A. D. **Selected Essays.** Translated by Frances Burnce from the Hebrew Edition by N. Teradyon and A. Shohat, with a Biographical Sketch by E. Silberschlag. 1938

Ha-Am, Achad (Asher Ginzberg). **Ten Essays on Zionism and Judaism.** Translated from the Hebrew by Leon Simon. 1922. New Introduction by Louis Jacobs

Halevi, Jehudah. **Selected Poems of Jehudah Halevi.** Translated into English by Nina Salaman, Chiefly from the Critical Text Edited by Heinrich Brody. 1924

Heine, Heinrich. **Heinrich Heine's Memoir:** From His Works, Letters, and Conversations. Edited by Gustav Karpeles; English Translation by Gilbert Cannan. 1910. Two volumes in one

Heine, Heinrich. **The Prose Writings of Heinrich Heine.**
Edited, with an Introduction, by Havelock Ellis. 1887

Hirsch, Emil G[ustav]. **My Religion.** Compilation and
Biographical Introduction by Gerson B. Levi. **Including
The Crucifixion Viewed from a Jewish Standpoint:** A Lecture
Delivered by Invitation Before the "Chicago Institute for
Morals, Religion and Letters." 1925/1908

Hirsch, W. **Rabbinic Psychology:** Beliefs about the Soul
in Rabbinic Literature of the Talmudic Period. 1947

Historical Views of Judaism: Four Selections. 1973

Ibn Gabirol, Solomon. **Selected Religious Poems of Solomon Ibn
Gabirol.** Translated into English Verse by Israel Zangwill
from a Critical Text Edited by Israel Davidson. 1923

Jacobs, Joseph. **Jesus as Others Saw Him:** A Retrospect
A. D. 54. Preface by Israel Abrahams; Introductory Essay by
Harry A. Wolfson. 1925

Judaism and Christianity: Selected Accounts, 1892-1962.
1973. New Preface and Introduction by Jacob B. Agus

Kohler, Kaufmann. **The Origins of the Synagogue and
The Church.** Edited, with a Biographical Essay by H. G. Enelow.
1929

Maimonides Octocentennial Series, Numbers I-IV. 1935

Mann, Jacob. **The Responsa of the Babylonian Geonim as a
Source of Jewish History.** 1917-1921

Maritain, Jacques. **A Christian Looks at the Jewish Question.** 1939

Marx, Alexander. **Essays in Jewish Biography.** 1947

Mendelssohn, Moses. **Phaedon; or, The Death of Socrates.**
Translated from the German [by Charles Cullen]. 1789

Modern Jewish Thought: Selected Issues, 1889-1966. 1973.
New Introduction by Louis Jacobs

Montefiore, C[laude] G. **Judaism and St. Paul:** Two Essays. 1914

Montefiore, C[laude] G. **Some Elements of the Religious
Teaching of Jesus According to the Synoptic Gospels.** Being
the Jowett Lectures for 1910. 1910

Radin, Max. **The Jews Amongs the Greeks and Romans.** 1915

Ruppin, Arthur. **The Jews in the Modern World.** With an
Introduction by L. B. Namier. 1934

Smith, Henry Preserved. **The Bible and Islam;** or, The Influence
of the Old and New Testaments on the Religion of Mohammed.
Being the Ely Lectures for 1897. 1897

Stern, Nathan. **The Jewish Historico-Critical School of the
Nineteenth Century.** 1901

Walker, Thomas [T.] **Jewish Views of Jesus:** An Introduction
and an Appreciation. 1931. New Introduction by Seymour Siegel

Walter, H. **Moses Mendelssohn:** Critic and Philosopher. 1930

Wiener, Leo. **The History of Yiddish Literature in the
Nineteenth Century.** 1899

Wise, Isaac M. **Reminiscences.** Translated from the German and
Edited, with an Introduction by David Philipson. 1901